WHAT TO READ IN
THE RAIN

2012

WHAT TO READ IN
THE RAIN

AN ANTHOLOGY OF WRITING FROM 826 SEATTLE
BY FAMOUS AND NOT-YET-FAMOUS ADULT AND YOUNG WRITERS

8 2 6
SEATTLE

826 Seattle
8414 Greenwood Ave. N.
Seattle, Washington, 98103, USA, Earth, Sol, Via Lactea
www.826seattle.org
206-725-2625

ISBN 0-9779832-9-3

Editor: Bill Thorness
Designer: Jacob Covey | Unflown Design
Printer: Thomson-Shore, Dexter, Michigan

Special thanks to Amazon.com for helping fund this project.

In Memory of Kim Ricketts

(1957 – 2011)

whose brilliance and boundless energy helped launch
what we fondly call our "Hotel Book."

CONTENTS

CONTENTS

CONNECTIONS

ABOUT 826 SEATTLE

A 2011 finalist for the National Youth Arts and Humanities Award

At 826 Seattle we match young people and their volunteer adult mentors in our writing lab, located behind the Greenwood Space Travel Supply Company* where together they inspire, teach, write, edit, learn, rewrite, redraft, tutor, invent, and imagine stories, poems, essays, jokes, songs, plays, comics, blogs, invitations, personal statements, job applications, and recipes. All of our programs and tutoring are free of charge to the youth of Seattle.

In our culture, the ability to communicate effectively in writing opens large doors.

Everybody does better when everybody does better.

*FOR DETAILS, PLEASE SEE P. 223

Tom Robbins is an 826 Seattle Board Member and author of nine novels, including *Fierce Invalids Home from Hot Climates,* and *Villa Incognito.*

How Far Is Far Out?

TOM ROBBINS

WHEN I RECEIVED my copy of the most recent book of stories by the young writers of 826 Seattle, I was immediately pleased by its title, *Adventures in Reading*, for reading can be—and probably should be—an adventure. Writing, however, is an even greater adventure, because the reader can only go where the writer has gone before her. If the adventurous reader is a traveler, the adventurous writer is an explorer.

The best writing adventures begin like this: You pack your talent, your ambition, your inspiration, your imagination, your sense of humor, your curiosity, your research, your life experience—and a bottle—into your little canoe and push out onto the vast and savage ocean and see where the currents take you.

Oh, yeah, about that bottle: Did I mention that there's a genie in it? There is—and while nobody knows this genie's name or place of origin, he's believed to have entered our world on that momentous occasion when language was first turned-on by the seductive wiggles and flirtatious eyelash-batting of style.

Language was humankind's first invention and remains both its most useful and its most grandiose. While our initial utterances would certainly have been monosyllabic references to such elemental features as hunger or cold or mother, it would not have been long, by the clock of pre-history, before the spellbinding power and transportive beauty of language would have been recognized and incorporated into prevailing ritual systems. The shaman's invocation became tribal chant became family prayer became personal opinion and private flapdoodle.

Whatever the nature or substance of that first nonfunctional word that wriggled like a startled butterfly out of the muddy cocoon of a Paleolithic grunt, the first *sentence* ever spoken was, undoubtedly, "Tell me a story." Not, "What's for dinner, Honey?" or "Have a nice day." or "I'll see you in court." or "How much is that saber-toothed tiger in the window?" It was, "Tell me a story."

We define ourselves through narration, and it wasn't until we could tell stories about our lives that we could even begin to understand our lives. It was only a matter of time, however, before social comprehension was not enough; we longed to understand the psyche, the universe, the cosmos; and since our direct experiences with elements of such magnitude and complexity were at best ambiguous, we had to imagine them.

Once imagination was born, there was no limit to the stories that might be told or to the linguistic forms employed in their telling. And it was thus that style commenced its complicated but enduring love affair with language. Once our brighter ancestors came to appreciate that the words assembled to tell a story could be equally as important as the story itself, that, often enough, language *is* the story—that language is not the frosting but the cake—the genie appeared. The genie waved a green flag and announced in his big genie voice: "Let the adventure begin!!"

Okay, but just how adventurous does our writing dare be? Can we agree with Stanley Elkin, a most wonderful novelist, who said: "The furthest out you can go is the best place to be."? Or with Albert Einstein who, though not much of writer, was a fairly smart cookie, and who advised: "Go out as far as you can go—and start from there."? And what about the celebrated Spanish poet Juan Ramón Jiménez, who exhorted, "If they give you ruled paper, write the other way."?

Speaking only for myself and having good reason to suspect that I'm in a minority, I'm for writing that is willing not merely to record, but to transform, writing that is willing to wrap itself in the chiffon of dream and the goatskin of myth, but that shuns the mummy bandages of good old academic realism because it can't tolerate the smell of formaldehyde. I'm for writing that cannot be intimidated or usurped by <u>any</u> ideology; writing that has the wisdom to admit that much of life is disputably goofy and that has the guts to treat that goofiness as seriously as it treats suffering and despair.

I'm for writing that sings in the shower. I'm for writing that shoplifts lingerie from Victoria's Secret and climbs up on the roof at night to look for UFOs. I'm for writing that quivers on your lap like a saucer of Jell-O and runs up your leg like a mouse. I'm for writing that knocks holes in library walls. I'm for writing that calls its own number, on a telephone line made from the nose hairs of Buddha. I'm for writing that shall fear no evil, lo though it walk through the valley of the shadow of lit crit. I'm for salty writing, itchy writing, steel-belted, copper-bottomed, nickel-plated writing, writing that attends the white lilacs after the heat has gone. I'm for writing that rescues the princess—*and* the dragon. I'm for writing that runs with the women who run with the wolves, and does belly-flops into waters infested with dangling participles.

I'm for writing that glugs out of the deep unconscious like ketchup from a bottle; writing that can get drunk on ketchup as well as on champagne; drunk writing!, intoxicated by beauty and ugliness alike—but as scornful of mediocrity as if it were a hairball coughed up by a poisoned cat.

I'm for writing that can wop it, bop it, or rock it; sing it, wing it, or ring-ding-a-ding it, that smears its hair with cocoa butter and goes Ommmmmmmmm. I'm for writing that resembles alchemy. I'm for writing that has an appetite! I'm for writing that's more Dizzy than Gillespie and more Thelonius than Monk; writing that can sail little paper airplanes over the moon and cause a blue dolphin to leap from a sink of dirty dishes—but has absolutely no interest in saving you fifteen percent on your car insurance.

And lastly, I'm for writing that lets the genie out of the bottle. Remember that little canoe that you've pushed out onto the vast and savage ocean? Well, the genie can turn that canoe into a magic carpet. You will, of course, want to climb aboard, but before you fly away to the ancient cities or brand new planets of your choice, be sure to circle Seattle—to circle it 826 times. Thank you, 826 Seattle! Happy adventuring to all of you.

WHAT TO READ IN
THE RAIN

Northwest Field Recording—WA (7 inch/A side), Victoria Haven, 2010

Courtesy of Victoria Haven and Greg Kucera Gallery, Seattle. © Victoria Haven

1

COMINGS
-&-
GOINGS

Photo by Alicia Craven.

Ben-Oni Eliezer Jean is eighteen years old and from Haiti. He loves his family, basketball, and his friends. In the future, he will be a professional basketball player.

Coffee in the Morning: Sometimes I Think of Haiti

BEN-ONI ELIEZER JEAN

I am from a two-story big warm house my family built.
From four big bedrooms, one living room, and one kitchen.
We have many aloe vera plants and some roses.
Some red, and some turned pink from the sun.
From a Haitian city, Port Au Prince, in the Caribbean.

I am from the heat season—summer in Haiti.
I spend almost all year in the heat.
Only December is just one little bit cold. Not like Seattle.
I come from a country with nine months of heat.
A country that has mountains like teeth.
When I lived back home, I saw the mountains far away.
From my roof—gray, green, black, and white.
I saw the beautiful night.

I am from College Mix Frere Alexandre.
It's a big school in the Haitian city of Nazon.
Four stories, the colors are green and white.

Twelve big classrooms, seven teachers.
I learned three languages in this school.
I learned French, English, and Spanish.
I met new students.

I am from Marché Carfour Payen.
It is a big market in Haiti.
You can find anything you want to cook
Like tomatoes, rice, black beans.
My mom cooked vegetables every day.
She never gets angry, that's why I like her.

I am from Champ de Mars.
A big place where I play soccer and basketball with my friends.
Sometimes my girlfriend and I go there. We play together.
We buy ice cream and eat together.

I am also from sweet mango juice,
Yellow banana smells, and green avocados, big as grapefruits.
From sweet watermelon juice—green outside, red inside.
Some papaya, pineapple, and peanuts.
They are very beautiful and sweet juices.

I am from "Souvient vos Demaint" (Remember you, tomorrow).
I always think about that and that
Motivates all the things I want or need to do.
That's why I learn more English,
And about what I want to do in my future to help my family.

I am from coffee every morning. It smells so good—
My mom, she makes it.
I'm so glad and I'm so very proud when
I wake up in the morning to drink the coffee before I go to school.
The coffee helps me learn more about what I want to do.

Photo by Michelle Quint.

Dave Eggers is the author of seven books including *Zeitoun*, and the founder and editor of independent publishing house McSweeney's. He co-founded the nonprofit writing and tutoring center 826 Valencia in San Francisco, and sister 826 centers have opened in seven other cities. Dave lives in the San Francisco Bay Area with his wife and two children.

Hitchhiker's Cuba

DAVE EGGERS

ON THE ROAD OUTSIDE HAVANA, where weeds grow through the train tracks, and the crumbling buildings, colors fading into a decorator's dream, alternate with wild trees and shrubs in the most gorgeous, postapocalyptic way, is where it first happened, when we first got an idea of how it all worked.

We had missed a turn (we suspected) and so had stopped to ask directions. We pulled over next to a median strip, on which stood eight or 10 people, half with shopping bags, presumably waiting for a bus. We rolled down the window, smiled sheepishly and directed our confusion to one of the men (tall, black, in a shiny Adidas jersey). With a swift sort of purpose, he nodded and stepped forward from the island and toward us, in a gesture we took as exceptionally friendly and helpful, getting so close to better relate the coordinates...

Then he was in the car. It happened before we knew it had happened. He just opened the door, and then suddenly he was giving us directions from within the car. The smallish back seat was empty, then full, full with this large man, his knees cramped up near his chin. He was so nonchalant, and had not uttered any commands or taken out a gun or any of the other ostensible signs of carjacking, and so it dawned on us that this was what happened in Rome. In Cuba, that is. Here hitchhiking is custom. Hitchhiking is essential. Hitchhiking is what makes Cuba move. All those other people on the median strip? All waiting for rides. Perhaps a bus, yes, if they have a few hours to lose. But until then there are cars, and occasionally the back of a bicycle, and the hope that someone will stop. So the man in our car tells us where we're going, and then we're off, eastbound, through the outer parts of Havana, along the train tracks, more and more green, past the heartbreaking roadside propaganda, 10 miles, 15 miles out of the city's center.

His name is Juan Carlos. And while he speaks a little English, thankfully in the passenger seat is a translator/navigator (T/N), and she duly interprets.

What does Juan Carlos do for a living?

He's a basketball player-coach.

Where are we taking him?

Home. Is that O.K.?

Of course, sure. Is he married?

Yes. Actually, he says, his wife is the starting center for the Cuban women's national basketball team. Do you want to meet her?

Hell, of course we want to meet her.

His building is a concrete complex overgrown with weeds and drying laundry. Neighbors stare from above, their arms draped over balconies. Through the door and inside Juan Carlos' apartment suddenly there is Judith, easily seven feet tall. Eight? She's huge. She leans down to offer her cheek for kisses. The walls are crowded with images of Michael Jordan. We say we're from Chicago. They nod politely. Juan Carlos thinks the Suns will take it this year. The Suns? We nod politely.

Judith is practicing for the Sydney Games, with her team playing against three other teams in the Cuban women's intramural league. From the four teams, the squad for the national team is chosen. Does she think she'll have any trouble making the team? She chuckles. Dumb question. No, she'll be starting.

They ask when we'll be back in Havana. We don't know. When you come back, they say, this is your home. Their in-laws live down the street, so they'll stay with them and we can have their bed. We say fine, but for now we have to move, must get back on the road (but not before getting a quick snapshot, for which Judith changes into her uniform), because we're heading up the coast, and we have more people to pick up and move, from here to there.

That becomes the point—it had not been the plan at the outset but now is the mission, one thrust upon us—the picking up of people, because, as we learn soon enough, the most common roadside scenery in Cuba, besides the horse-drawn wagons and broken-down classic American cars, is its hitchhikers. The roads are littered with people everywhere, along the huge highways and two-laners, all strewn with mothers and their daughters, grandmothers, working men, soldiers, teenagers, schoolchildren in their white, white shirts and mustard-colored pants or skirts, day and night, in the rain or otherwise. All waiting.

They wait for hours for the occasional bus or a spot on the back of a truck, waiting on the median strips, at the intersections, sitting with their possessions or on them, along the gravelly highway shoulders, patience their essence because gasoline is scarce and expensive, cars are owned by few and function for fewer, the buses are terrible and slow and always so full. And so we are driving in our Subaru, a tiny thing but big enough for five, and we're Americans come to move the Cubans from place to place. Feel our luxury! Hear our engine's roar!

Up the coast, and in ten minutes we stop for Jorge, who gets in at a stoplight and is going toward Varadero, a beach town on the north coast. Jorge is about eighteen, in khakis and a pink shirt, with a very hip-seeming haircut, freshly gelled, a kind of haircut that makes him look half monk, half member of a dancing, harmonizing teen quintet. Jorge's father, he says, left for the U.S. years ago. He was one of the so-called balseros, the rafters who left from the Bay of Mariel in 1994 during one of Castro's periodic spurts of permitted emigration. Now he's in Miami.

T/N: What does he do there?

Jorge: I don't know. I haven't talked to him since he left.

T/N: Oh, that's too bad.

Jorge: No, no. It's O.K.

We drop the subject of Dad of Jorge. We pass miles and miles of oil pumps along the ocean, some pumping, their bird heads rhythmically dipping their beaks, others inanimate, the surf spraying over. We ask Jorge what he does for a living. He says he's a student of astronomy.

"Oh, so what does that entail?" I ask the rear-view mirror. T/N translates.

"Oh, you know," he says. "Cervezas, sodas, comida..."

Oh. Ha. Not astronomy. Gastronomy. Big laughs all around. The sky is watercolor gray, and the clouds hold rain. We all go over the mix-up three more times. Not astronomy. Gastronomy. Yes. The beach comes into view, palm trees bent by a wicked ocean-borne wind. Jorge wants to know if we need some place to stay. Jorge, like every last man in Cuba, knows of just the place, the perfect casa particular—the Cuban version of a bed and breakfast—and he, like most, is very difficult to convince of one's lack of casa particular-based need.

No thanks, we say.

I know just the place, he says.

No thanks, we say.

Very nice place.

No thanks but—

Clean, very cheap.

Thanks, no.

Have your own kitchen, very private.

No, no.

Only $18.

You are too kind but—

You want me to show you?

We drop Jorge at the beach at Santa Maria del Mar and get back to moving down the coast. Minutes later we pull over for two girls, each carrying a cake, each about twenty, giggling to themselves in the back seat. Sisters? No, just friends. They're on their way home, to the next town, Guanabo. We pass a photo shoot, by the water: a skeletal blond woman, a photographer, a band of Cuban men, grinning in matching shirts, all standing in front of a mid-'50s Chevy, powder blue. We all wonder who the model is. Anyone we know? The girls giggle more. We're suddenly pals, they and all hitchers instantly familiar, completely at ease—as if we've picked up classmates on the way to the mini-mart. Safety here is assumed, trust a given. Where is there danger in Cuba? This is unclear.

Sand covers the road. We almost get blindsided by a mural-burdened van from Pastors for Peace. Bumper stickers thereon: END THE EMBARGO! ¡VAMOS A CUBA! Terrible drivers, these guys.

We drop the cake-bearing girls on the corner just past Guanabo's main drag and pick up a much older woman, sixty or so, who's been visiting her mother and needs to go just a little ways out of town. Ten minutes later— ¡Aqui, Aqui!—she gets out. She smiles thank-you, and we smile goodbye— and again we're empty. We don't like to be empty. Through the Cuban countryside we feel ashamed to have the back seat unpeopled—all this room we have, all this fuel. It's getting dark, and as the roads go black, what was a steady supply of hitchhikers, punctuating the roads like mile markers, quickly disappears. Where they go is unclear. What happens when night comes but a ride hasn't? It's a problem of basic math we cannot fathom: always there are more riders than rides, a ten-to-one ratio at best, so what are the odds that all riders will be transported before sunset?

At Varadero, there is money. Resorts and busloads of European tourists waiting impatiently in lobbies for their bags to be ported to their private beachside cabanas. There are buffets and games of water polo organized in the main pool—a ridiculous sort of comfort level for about $100 a night. (Best yet, the help is obsequious and a fifty-cent tip would do just fine!) After being turned away at the daunting gates of the massive Club Med, we drop our luggage next door and set out to the area's most fiery hot spot, the Cafe Havana, a huge disco/Hard Rock-style fun provider. The place is over-flowing with tourists from around the world, come to see how the Cubans entertain.

We sit at a table by the stage, and after some fantastic salsa-dancing action—women wearing little beyond sequins and feathers—there is a magician, ponytailed, with two ponytailed assistants. And this magician's specialty is doves. Everywhere he is making doves appear. From his sleeve, a dove. From a newspaper, a dove. A balloon is popped, and a dove appears and flaps wildly. The crowd loves it. The doves appear, each one flailing its wings for a few seconds of chaos and quasi-freedom. Then the magician, with fluid nonchalance, grabs the dove from the air, two-handed, making from the explosion of feathery white a smooth inanimate sculpture of a bird. Then in one swift motion he shoves the dove into a small cage, with little steel bars, on a stand by his waist. Once inside, the doves sit docilely, staring ahead through the tiny silver bars. Though there is a hole just behind them, they sit, cooing—one dove, then two, three, four, five, six, all in a row. When he is done, the magician is applauded. We all love him. The birds in their cage, content and so pretty. How does he do it? He is fantastic. Then the band comes on, and everyone dances.

The next day we're off, Varadero to Cienfuegos. First passengers, from a roadside crowd of fifteen or twenty: a mother-and-child duo, the mother skinny and snaggle-toothed, the baby perfect and in pink, eleven months old, little black shoes, shiny; they're headed home. We roll with them past horse-drawn wagons and slow, lanky cows. Egrets skim over the road, perpendicular. Air warm, sky overcast. The car screams.

They get out near Jovellanos, and we never get their names. In Jovellanos, a medium-size adobe town of narrow streets, we get lost, quickly and irrevocably. At a street corner, there appears beside us a man on a bicycle. He knows where to go, he says—just follow him. We rumble behind him and his bike at 15 m.p.h., the streets full of onlookers watching our parade—left turn, right, left, left, right, left, ten minutes and there we are, back on the main road. He points ahead, toward the on-ramp. Aha.

We pull up next to him. He is sweating profusely and grinning. We slip him $5—for many, we're told, that's almost a month's salary—because we are wealthy and glamorous Americans and we appreciate his help. So easy to change the quality, the very direction, of Cubans' lives! It seems possible that, between our ride sharing and tip giving, we can single-handedly redress whatever harm has been done. Oh, if only!

Just outside Jovellanos there's Estelle, chatty, about thirty-five, and her ten-year-old Javier, who jump in at a dusty corner. Estelle sighs and laughs as she gets in and says hello. Had they been waiting long? Yes, yes, she says, they'd been waiting an hour and a half. They're going to a town called Australia, twenty minutes away. "Why is there a town in Cuba called Australia?" we ask. Estelle doesn't know. She turns to Javier. Javier has no idea. She shrugs and smiles.

We dodge more wagons, their drivers frequently asleep, the donkeys as sad as donkeys insist on appearing. There are men in uniform waiting for rides. There are women with groceries and babies waiting for rides. Some of the hitchers raise their hands to a passing car, but most don't. Some express frustration when they feel that a passing car could fit more people (i.e., them), but most don't. Most just watch you pass, squinting beyond you, for the next slowing car or truck. But when a car stops, never is there competition for the ride. Never is there shoving or even the most mild sort of disagreement. Each time we pull over, whoever's closest simply walks to the car and gets in. There is no system in place for the rewarding of longest wait, or oldest, or most pregnant. It's both perfectly fair and completely random.

We drop Estelle and Javier in Australia and pick up a family just outside of town. Grandfather, mother, daughter. They had been visiting a friend at the hospital and are going where we're going, to Playa Giron, home of the Cuban monument to the heroes of the Bay of Pigs. Our merengue tape, bought at a gas station, tinkles quietly from the speakers. We offer them—we offer everyone—water, cookies, crackers. They decline, and like most riders, this family says nothing unless we speak first; they don't even talk to one another. They watch the countryside pass, content. We are surprised, with them and most riders, that they do not want to know where we're from. Why are they not curious about us, the Americans here to save them? At their house, a bent-over salmon-colored ranch on a brown-dirt street, they ask us if we'd like to come in for a cold drink. We decline, must move. They scoot out. In the process, the daughter's shoe catches on the seat and loses its heel. She looks up, embarrassed, horrified. "New shoes too," says Mom. We all chuckle and then sigh. Kids.

After Giron, we're headed to Cienfuegos, through more fields of tobacco, then bananas. When night comes again, there are no streetlights, no lights anywhere, and on the winding two-lane roads, the avoidance of donkey carts and tractors and people requires tremendous, arcadelike hand-eye coordination. All is dark, and then things will suddenly be in front of us, lit as if by a camera's flash; swerving is an essential skill. Up ahead a car is parked, hazards blinking. There is a group of people around the car. Obviously an ambush. We should not stop. In the U.S., we would not stop.

We stop. Four people are standing around a white, early-'70s Volvo. They're out of gas; can we help? Yes, yes, we say, of course. They want to siphon from our tank. They have an actual siphon right there. We don't have enough, we say, noticing that we're almost out ourselves. We'll take them to the next town. Another man, Esteban, about nineteen, gets in the back seat, as does Marisa, twenty-four, petite, in silk blouse and black jeans. They hold the gas container on their laps. It's fifteen minutes to tiny-town Roda and its one-pump gas station.

As we wait, we talk to Marisa, who we learn is studying English; she wants to get into tourism. She is married to an American, a photographer from Los Angeles. She was just coming back from Havana, as a matter of fact, where she was seeing him off at the airport.

So who are the others in the car?

She doesn't know. It's a taxi.

A taxi? A taxi running out of gas?

Big laughs all around.

The taxi was taking three passengers the three hours from Havana to Cienfuegos; the driver had grossly miscalculated how much fuel that would require. They had left at three that afternoon. It was now at least nine. We fill up their container and are ready to go.

But the Subaru won't start. It won't even turn over. In a flash, Esteban is out of the car and pushing. I'm driving, and he's barking orders, which need to be translated instantaneously by T/N. I have no idea what we're doing. We stop. Esteban, sighing loudly, takes my place, and then I'm pushing. Down the road, and before long we're out of the town and into the dark fields. The road is red from the taillights and slippery and I can't get a grip, but then boom, Esteban pops the clutch and the Subaru whinnies and I get in while it's moving and we're off, Esteban at the wheel. Like a getaway car! In a minute Esteban's doing 80 m.p.h. He's veering on and off the road. "¡Flojo! ¡Flojo!" Marisa is saying, urging him to slow down, but young Esteban has something to prove to her and to T/N, so eighty it is, the engine hitting high notes with full vibrato.

We get to the taxi. They fill up the Volvo while we wait. We meet the third passenger, Dale, an English-speaking med student from St. Kitts, who decides he's sick of speaking Spanish, so he'll ride to Cienfuegos with us. He's studying Spanish there, the first year of seven he'll spend in Cuba on his way to a medical degree. We follow the taxi into Cienfuegos, drop off Dale at his barbed wire-surrounded dormitory, check into a hotel with red light bulbs and a lounge singer plowing through the high points of the Billy Joel songbook, and we're done for the night.

In the morning, on the way to the town of Trinidad, it's all rolling hills and farms, and the people have been waiting for us. At an intersection ten miles out of Cienfuegos we stop at a gathering of twenty or so, mostly young men, some in uniform. One gets in, followed by a woman, running—she's just jumped out of another car and into ours. Her name is Maela and, like the vast majority of Cuban women, Maela is a devout spandex enthusiast. She's in a black-and-white bodysuit, bisected with belt, and she's laughing like mad at her car-to-car coup, the soldiers tossing her a wide variety of obscene gestures as we drive away. The soldier we've got is named Jordan; he's doing the mandatory military service—two years—and is heading home for the weekend. Maela was in Cienfuegos with friends and is going home too. He's quiet, but she's bubbly, and through the countryside we roll.

Ten miles and Jordan gets out at a tiny town called Pepito, where Condela gets in. Condela is about forty-five and has crumbs all over his mouth and hands—he has been eating a pastry while waiting for a ride, standing just outside a bakery. He's a butcher in Trinidad, so he'll be with us the rest of the ride, about an hour more. Condela has been visiting friends and is on his way back home. He asks where we're from. Los Estados Unidos, we say. Ah, he says. He has family in Miami. (Everyone has family in Miami.)

We drop off Maela; she giggles thanks, and in comes Belgis, about forty, pregnant, in a white frilly blouse and floral spandex leggings. She was waiting for three hours. She was visiting her family, and is on her way to Playa Yaguardabo to see her in-laws, ten minutes up the road. We get there, and she's out. Condela stays put and seems perturbed—the back seat is not so big—when we welcome a young couple, Alexander and Yaineris, who bustle in, exhaling with relief. They have a chicken with them. A live chicken. Condela laughs at our surprise. The chicken is small and in a plastic bag—its red, confused little head poking out. Alexander and Yaineris are married, and have been visiting her parents; they're headed back home to Trinidad. The ocean is a few hills to our right. Tour buses whip past us doing 75 m.p.h. The tour buses are always empty, always doing seventy-five, and they don't stop for anyone.

Halfway to Trinidad, while we are passing La Guira, something recklessly symbolic happens. At the bottom of a small valley, there is a split second when a huge, bulbous green army truck passes us, heading in the other direction. At the same instant, we are passing on our right a straw-hatted farmer on horseback and, to our left, a woman on a bicycle. Symbolism contained: each of our vehicles represents a different element of what makes Cuba Cuba. The bicycle (1) is the Cubans' resourcefulness and symbiosis with their communist brethren (about a million bikes were donated by the Chinese, decades ago). The army truck (2) is the constant (though relatively sedate and casual, we'd say) military presence. We are the tourists (3), perhaps the future, our dollars feeding into Cuba's increasingly dominant second economy, largely inaccessible to Cuba's proletariat; and the horseback farmer (4) represents, of course, the country's rural backbone. All caught, for one split second, on a single linear plane.

Fun!

At Trinidad, a colonial town 400 years old, sun bleached and ravishing, we drop off Condela. He shows us his shop, right on the main cobblestone drag. "If you need anything," he says, pointing to a storefront, "I'm right here." Trinidad is much too perfectly aged and brilliantly colored to be free of tourists: Germans, Spanish, Italians, even a few Americans drawling Indiana r's.

On to Sancti Spiritus. Carlos, about thirty, and Armena, twenty-five, get in just outside Trinidad, where three dozen others are waiting with them.

Carlos works in construction now, after a five-year stint as a policeman in Havana. Armena has been in Trinidad looking for work.

"What kind of work?"

"Anything at all," she says.

"Is it hard to find work?"

Eyes are rolled. Yes, yes. These days, yes. We drop off Armena at a little yellow house, clothes hanging in the windows. Carlos gets out soon after. At Banao, a tiny town, there is a crowd of forty waiting; a dozen or so people wave us down. We can't stop right in the middle—too confusing. (Oh, to have a bus!) We drive to the end, where the throng thins. We nod to a woman, and she jogs forward and gets in. Dayami is about thirty, lipsticked, in tight black jeans with a black mesh shirt over a sports bra. She's a doctor, on her way to pick up her daughter at school. We ask if it's hard to get medicine. After all, on the way from Havana, a billboard had read: YANKEE EMBARGO: GENOCIDE AGAINST CUBA. She says no, not really.

We pass a barefoot, shirtless boy on the back of a donkey. A mile later, a man on horseback, galloping, beams as we go by, takes his hat off and waves it to us in mid-gallop, even as we're passing him going 65 m.p.h. Is Cuba cinematic? It is.

At a corner outside the city, we grab a tallish, red-haired woman in a white medical jacket. When she gets in, she and Dayami laugh. They used to work together, and begin chatting. She's a dentist, and had loaned her bike to a friend. We drop Dayami off at her daughter's school and park in Sancti Spiritus' central square. A school band practices in an auditorium above us. Mopeds buzz to and fro, soldiers talk to schoolchildren, and within minutes we see the dentist. She rides by on her bicycle and rings her bell. "I got my bike back!" she sings to us. Cuba has become one huge Richard Scarry neighborhood.

Then we're off to Santa Clara, too dark to pick up anyone, but the next day it's Santa Clara to Havana, and en route there is Wendy. Wendy is talkative and insists on tapping T/N on the shoulder and saying "¡Mira!" (Look here!) every time she has a question or statement. She's married, has a three-year-old, works at a peso food market. "Oh, I knew you weren't Cuban," she says. Why? we ask.

"Cuban couples won't pick people up," she says. "People in groups or driving alone but never couples."

(Shoulder poke) "¡Mira!": she has family in New York, New Jersey.

(Shoulder poke) "¡Mira!": she also cleans houses, to make ends meet.

(Shoulder poke) "¡Mira!": "You know how the situation in Cuba is, right?"

She's on her way home. Her husband's in prison, she says—she has just been visiting him. He was convicted, with nine others, of stealing gasoline. He was originally sentenced to four years, but with a lawyer—he is innocent, was set up, she insists—he was able to get the sentence reduced to twenty months. She gets out and is replaced by a cheerful trio—a large blond woman, her sister and her sister's daughter. Havana? they ask. Yes, yes. Oh, they cannot believe their luck. They cannot believe they're getting a ride all the way to Havana. Waiting long? Hours. Are things always like this? Getting worse every year. Castro, they say, is getting too old, senile maybe. Things are not good. Are we aware of the situation here? Things are getting worse. The past ten years, they say, much worse. Fidel is obsessed with the U.S., they say, which is fine, but he must start taking care of things here at home. When we drop them off, at about noon, they're astounded that they're home before nightfall. They are beside themselves. When we're in Cuba again, they tell us, we have a home, we have a family. We take pictures.

And finally, there is Yuricema. About twenty, dark brown skin, wide white smile. She gets in on the Malecon, just shy of the Hemingway Marina. She's coming home from school; she's a business and law student. We're in the suburbs of Havana, and the sky is purplish and getting darker as we approach the city's center. Yuricema claims that her English is bad, but then she speaks it, and it's kind of perfect, at least in terms of the words she does know. The accent sounds more California than Havana. We ask her where she learned English.

"My professor was Michael Bolton," she says.

I almost veer off the road.

"Michael Bolton?" T/N says.

"Yes, yes, he is very good. I love him."

Is it possible? Was Michael Bolton ever a teacher of English in Cuba? We hit the main drag of the Malecon. The ocean is bursting against the wall, spraying the waves up and over the road, thirty feet high. It's almost dark. T/N wants one more shot at it.

"So, wait, Michael Bolton was your English teacher?"

Yuricema bursts out laughing. We laugh too. She asks T/N the English word for "¡Ojala!" T/N translates, "I wish!"

She had been trying to say "My preference is Michael Bolton" but said instead "My professor is..." She had one of his albums, but she loaned it to a friend, and then he claimed never to have seen it. Yuricema rolls her eyes to underline how stupid her friend is. We offer to send her a new Michael Bolton tape. I throw in that we'll send her whatever Michael Bolton stuff we can find. Posters, books, everything. "Very easy," I say. So easy to send wonderful things from America! She is beside herself. She gives T/N a pre-emptive gift—a wallet-size plastic calendar featuring an advertisement for a new kind of Vaseline. We thank her. I picture the sending of the Bolton care package. She will be so happy. She will never forget us. No one will ever forget us. Cuba will not forget us. We will come back, with not only the Michael Bolton stuff but a bigger car. No, a fleet of cars—and buses. We will sneak into the country from America, this time with legions of drivers—there are more of us coming all the time; it's getting so easy, embargo or no—and with enough buses and cars to get everyone everywhere they need to go. With our dollars and new tires, we will empty the roadsides and move the people place to place. The cars and buses will be huge and shiny, and we will flood the roads with them, get this place going—faster and faster, no more waiting for anything. Cars for everyone! We'll bring in some trains maybe. Hovercrafts, monorails. It'll be great. And all we'll ask in return is some hearty thanks and a nice beach to enjoy when we're in the neighborhood.

We wind our way through the dark streets of Old Havana, as Yuricema directs us to her home. When we get there we realize she lives a block from our hotel, the Hambos Mundos, a bargain at $120 a night. She gets out of the car and asks if we'd like to come in. We decline. She smiles.

"Don't forget me," Yuricema says, getting out and backing into her doorway. "Because I will never forget you."

Oh, just you wait, Yuricema. You haven't seen the last of us.

This story was originally published in TIME Magazine, Monday, Dec. 27, 1999.

Photo by Beth Harrington.

Photo by Scott Engelhardt.

David Lasky has created a number of critically acclaimed comic books, including a nine page mini-adaptation of Joyce's *Ulysses*. He is currently at work on a graphic novel about the Carter Family.

Lisa Maslowe lives in Seattle where she has been a comics artist, zinester, DJ, and bookseller. She is the house DJ for the Rat City Roller Girls, and is currently training to work as an aircraft mechanic.

This morning I woke up from an intense dream. I was showing you around Los Angeles where I grew up. I was telling you this:

WORDS : LISA MASLOWE
COMICS : DAVID LASKY

WE'D START ARRIVING AT THE BEACH AND THERE WOULD BE A BLACK BALL UP SIGNIFYING THAT THE WATER WASN'T SAFE.

AN ORGANIZATION STARTED UP IN SANTA MONICA, AND WE HAD A BRANCH AT OUR HIGH SCHOOL, IT WAS CALLED HEAL THE BAY.

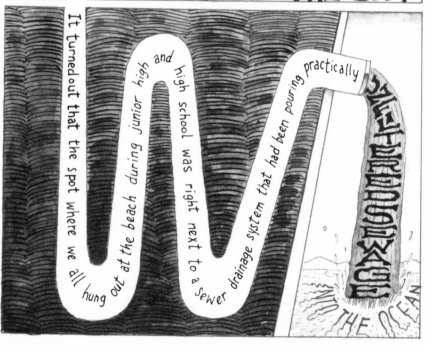

It turned out that the spot where we all hung out at the beach during junior high and high school was right next to a sewer drainage system that had been pouring practically UNTREATED SEWAGE INTO THE OCEAN.

THE OCEAN HAS A BRAIN

BY THE TIME I CAME BACK FROM MY FIRST YEAR OF COLLEGE, THE BEACH WAS LIKE AN OUTDATED & ABANDONED MOVIE LOT.

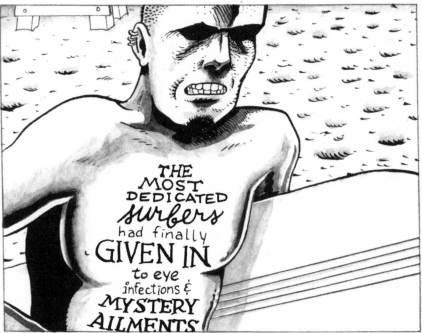

THE MOST DEDICATED *surfers* had finally GIVEN IN to eye infections & MYSTERY AILMENTS

IF THEY SURFED THEY HAD TO DO IT OUTSIDE of LosAngeles--
UP IN MALIBU, OR DOWN IN HUNTINGTON BEACH.

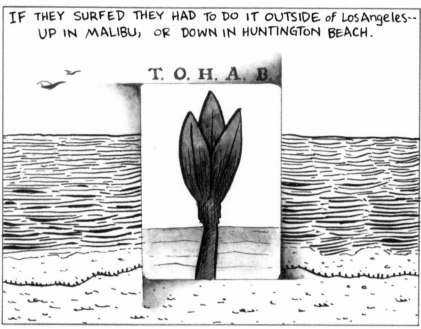

THE OCEAN HAS A BRAIN

WHAT TO READ IN THE RAIN

THE OCEAN HAS A BRAIN

WHAT TO READ IN THE RAIN

I returned to my childhood this morning in my dream.
Everything I expected was no longer there.

But somehow there were beautiful things
I couldn't have known about.

I decided to write a
poem about this.

I couldn't get past
the first line:

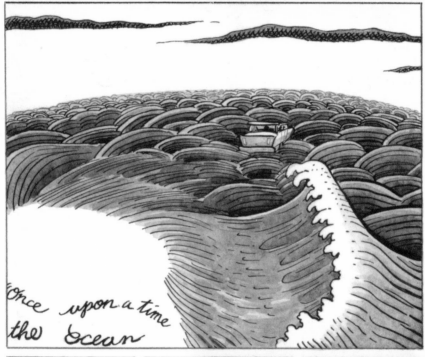

Once upon a time
the Ocean

THE OCEAN HAS A BRAIN

Photo by Steve Case.

Margot Kahn's first book, *Horses That Buck*, is the biography of rodeo cowboy Bill Smith and his vanishing West. It won the High Plains Book Awards in 2009. When it rains, she likes to wrap herself in a blanket and get lost in a book set somewhere hot (*One Hundred Years of Solitude*), dry (*Plainsong*) or rainy (*The Highest Tide*), depending on her mood. She also loves to bake cookies when it rains and walk in the park with her family all under one giant umbrella.

Out of Ohio

MARGOT KAHN

IT ALL STARTED IN HIGH SCHOOL, over things we shouldn't have had but were easily gotten: bottles of Zima, cigarettes, and a little weed. The question wasn't what we were going to do, but where we were going to go. A few of us had ideas; others, like me, just knew we wanted out. Ohio, it felt to us, was too boring, too quiet, too bland. There was water, but it wasn't the ocean; there were forests, but no mountains; there was night-life, but none for us to partake in, except for one bar on the Coventry strip where you could go to hear mediocre live music and that never checked ID. We were kids stuck in the middle, wishing we were more extreme and, as such, more interesting. We wished we were cosmopolitan, or we wished we were farmers. We wished we were anything but good, clean Midwestern teenagers living in safe, suburban digs.

My home life was far from horrible. I had what I considered to be a fairly typical arrangement with my parents. They stayed out of my room, for the most part, and told me a few times a week to make my bed. My mother disapproved of half my wardrobe and most of my friends, but still usually let me out of the house and welcomed my surly pals in. I hung out at coffee shops and, on occasion, told my folks I would be at a coffee shop when in fact I was hanging out at someone's house while their parents were out of town. At Andy's we'd nip off his dad's bottles of scotch and Joel would play some jazz riffs on the baby grand piano; at Stephanie's, we'd sit in the back yard smoking all-natural cigarettes; at Nellie's we'd build bonfires and talk about the Beat poets and Che Guevera and foment revolution. Wherever we were we'd look up at the stars and pronounce our big dreams into the night. One night Andy shed his clothes into the dewy grass of his front yard and took off running down the road, right down the dotted yellow line, and we all followed him as if we would somehow be born again to someplace new.

Jack Kerouac's *On the Road* was a back-pocket textbook for our gang. A few of us had access to cars and they felt like sacred freedom machines. It was possible, at any moment, to scrape together gas money and light out for somewhere, anywhere else. We could be in New York City by morning if we drove through the night! And somehow, just knowing that we *could* was enough to tide us over. Instead, we drove our own roads a little too fast and tried to feel in control of our destinies. We listened to Pink Floyd and Miles Davis, Nine Inch Nails and The Cure, Phish and The Grateful Dead. We thought, in a not-so-intentional way, about escape and surrender. We thought about how to live a life you wanted to be living instead of a life you felt stuck in. Those thoughts, it always seemed, led us out of Ohio.

For all of our transgressions and desires to be different, we were all bound for college. Brian and Pete were inspired by Kerouac and Ginsberg's time at Columbia; "The City," as they always referred to New York, was the only place they wanted to go. Jessica was practical and would go where there was opportunity; the best college she could get into was where she would land, regardless of where it lay outside of her home state. Andy wanted to go west, to fish in blue-water rivers and live in a yurt; he wanted to be the Gary Snyder of us, saving owls and the wildness in everything. I didn't have much in the way of a plan. New York was scary to me, too big and too bright. I wanted to go someplace I could get lost but wouldn't feel lost, somewhere I would feel safe but not hemmed in. The way Andy talked about the West inspired me to go see if for myself. Maybe, I thought, that was where I belonged.

The summer after my sophomore year of high school, I took a trip to Wyoming and I was sold on the West. Everything was so grand and striking—the mountains, the clouds—and seemed to go on forever. Two years later, I spent three summer weeks hiking in Washington's North Cascades with a group of kids from across the country and here I fell in love. I loved the way the mountains looked at dusk and dawn, rolling out like waves; I loved the evergreen trees that covered all but their rocky summits; I appreciated that there were no poisonous snakes, no grizzly bears, no moose. These mountains were flush with water and had plenty of shade. Meadows of wildflowers, snow-capped peaks, and lake upon quiet lake were nestled snugly amongst the trees. I felt comfortable and comforted, awestruck and inspired. I didn't want to leave.

At the end of that hiking trip, my tripmates and I spent a few hours in Seattle's Pioneer Square. We sat on one of the benches near the pergola and ate slices of pizza off of paper plates. We watched the buses and the crazy people go by. We thought it was the coolest place we'd ever been—even the girl from New York City had to admit it. I said to myself that someday I wanted to live here, but it didn't happen right away. I wound up in Maine for college and spent my summers in various East Coast places with my new East Coast friends; but when graduation rolled around, the time was ripe. My roommate and I lit out for Seattle in late summer, crashed in her cousins' basement and lived out of our suitcases for three days until we found an apartment. She had a job, which was lucky because I did not; in order to sign the lease, at least one of us had to have proof of some income.

When I moved to Seattle, my parents didn't know what to tell their friends. Although Nirvana, the grunge scene, and Microsoft had been on the national radar for more than a few years, my folks weren't impressed.

People in Ohio had only vaguely heard of Seattle. It was as if I was moving to Greenland, or Mars. "What is she going to do there?" they would ask my mother. Or worse, they'd act like I had died, like she'd never see me again. It made me feel a little like a terrible daughter, and a little like a bold and brave explorer. At the time, I didn't have any kind of a life plan; I had no idea how long I was going to stay in Seattle or where I would go from here. The idea of "making a life" somewhere, of setting down roots, was far from my mind. I did feel strangely connected to the place rather immediately—walking the neighborhood streets and smiling at people who passed, shopping for groceries and delighting in random eucalyptus plants spilling over onto sidewalks. Live eucalyptus! My mother used to keep some dried stems in a vase on our dining table, but I'd never seen a live plant growing anywhere, let alone in someone's simple front yard.

I quickly made friends with a gaggle of other Midwest transplants— kids from Indiana, Illinois and Ohio—who lived in an apartment down the street. We'd tramp back and forth in our pajamas with pots of soup and VHS tapes tucked under our arms. I found a job writing obituaries for a local paper and another job selling tickets in the box office of a local theater. Everywhere I went or worked, I'd meet someone from Ohio. I started to wonder if anyone in Seattle was actually from here, and at the same time how anyone was still left in my home state. I was born in Cincinnati and raised in Cleveland because my immigrant grandparents had settled there and my parents went to state schools, found jobs, and raised a family. But for my generation, moving to a different city, state, or country became as easy as moving to the next county. Where our grandparents had to pack in steamer trunks and take slow boats across the ocean, the price of an airplane ticket for us was affordable and travel was fast. Jobs were so plentiful you could move first and worry about employment later. And with a laptop in your apartment or a few bucks at an Internet café, you could be in touch with your family and friends around the world—instantly. Within a few years, this new-found freedom that my generation discovered meant that my parents would watch all their children scatter across the country from Ohio, to California, Washington, Illinois, New York, and Pennsylvania.

A few years after I arrived in Seattle, I moved to New York to further my career. But instead of telling people I was from Ohio, I started saying I was from Seattle. Everyone would smile broadly and be impressed. "How cool!" they'd say. Once again, Seattle felt like a wild-west hinterland, almost as out there as Alaska. The reaction I got was a far cry from saying I was from Ohio and meeting with a bored, blank, apologetic expression. And instead of feeling fake, it felt more accurate to pin myself to the city I had chosen. If the place I lived was going to define me, Seattle was more my speed: a little rugged, a little nerdy, not to glitzy but not too backwoods, either. People from Seattle were friendly, arty, adventurous. It was exactly who I wanted to be. People from Ohio were, what? Flat, steady, earnest? Deep down, I acknowledged that was a part of me as well—and that I missed the strange humidity and lightning bugs of summer, the crispness of fall and the changing colors of the leaves, the bridges across the Cuyahoga and the tycoon mansions along Millionaire's Row, the feel of the cobblestone streets underfoot in Little Italy and the smell of the galleries in the art museum, the big lawn overlooking Chagrin Falls and the quiet rivers clogged with water lilies— but I didn't want it to define me entirely.

After my spell of higher education in New York, I returned to Seattle with the intention of staying. I married a guy from Tacoma, bought a house, and started a family. I will never be thought of as a native here, even if I stay for another fifty years, but it makes me happy that my son will be able to say he's from Seattle; I like to think I've given him a leg up on life right from the start. Of course, by the time he graduates from college, the cool place to be from might actually be Mars. Or maybe, just maybe, Ohio.

Photo by Chet Hay.

Isayas Bikila is ten years old and attends Northgate Christian Academy. He is very fast. He likes to read Geronimo Stilton books when it rains, or else watch movies. His biggest adventure so far has been traveling to Ethiopia.

A Walk At Deception Pass

ISAYAS BIKILA

CHAPTER 1

ONE DAY I WAS WALKING out of the woods and into the fog at Deception Pass, holding my umbrella in the rain. While I was walking, I heard a sound coming from the woods. It was getting louder and louder, and I smelled raspberries, so I had a weird idea that it was a raspberry monster that could fly. I made a run for it! When I looked back, I saw a flying monster! Its eyes and ears had raspberries. The monster was flying closer and closer to me. When he finally caught up, he kicked me on the back, and I fell off the bridge, into the fog at Deception Pass.

CHAPTER 2

WHEN I WAS FALLING DOWN
                              down
                                          down, I thought I would fall on hard ground, but when I looked, all I saw was water. I was *ZOOMING* straight into the water! I held my umbrella down (what a bad idea) and, when I got

to the water, I swam deep down to see the fish. While I was looking at the fish, a huge fish frightened me. His face was purple, his eyes green, his fins yellow, his mouth red. I had no time to swim away before that fish gulped me in his throat. Written in his throat were the words, "Welcome to the underworld where villains live."

I slid down his throat and into his stomach. "Oh great! Monsters for company—three of them!" The first one lunged at me with her sword. I didn't know what to do, so I held out my umbrella. To my surprise, blue and pink flames squirted from the umbrella at the monster. The monster screamed and burst into raspberry juice. The same thing happened to the other two monsters when I aimed my umbrella at them.

As I walked further down, I saw a small tunnel, which meant I had to crawl. While I was crawling, I noticed that the tunnel grew smaller and smaller, then bigger and bigger! I came to a stop when I saw a huge lava hole surrounded by monsters taking a class.

I had to get past them without falling in. I stuck my umbrella out, shooting three flames, turning three monsters into raspberry juice. When the teacher saw me, she flew toward me, caught me, and swung me around. Then she threw me toward a bomb, which blew my eyes out. My eyes and I fell into the lava, but the lava felt like water. I closed my eyelids, and when I opened them I was in bed.

Then I realized I had been dreaming. I had the feeling that a monster was under my bed, because it smelled like raspberries in my room, so I checked under my bed and saw... a cat.

Chapter 3

HOW DID A CAT get under my bed? I picked it up and put it outside. I made an angry face at it, and the cat grew larger. His teeth grew into fangs. The cat said, "No one has ever defeated ME!" I reached for my umbrella, but I remembered that the umbrella was in a dream. I ran and jumped on his head and pulled his hair out. He didn't feel anything. I ran back to my house, but he blew fire toward me, so I closed my eyes and opened them again.

Chapter 4

I WAS IN BED AGAIN. I had had two dreams. I dream too much. I got out and checked under my bed. Nothing. I looked outside, just rain. I knew I was fine. I decided to do the same thing I did in my dream: walk at Deception Pass. When I got there, I looked down. Just water. Today was a peaceful day.

Photo by Alicia Craven.

Nhut Truong is seventeen years old and from Vietnam. He loves his computer, his model toy Gundam 1/100 MG, and his girlfriend. In the future, he will have a good job, an all-mode Gundam 1/100 MG, and life will be easy with his girlfriend and his family.

Where I'm From

NHUT TRUONG

I WAS BORN IN VIETNAM, but we moved to America to start a new life. My experiences in both Vietnam and America make me who I am.

My dad was a soldier in the Vietnam Republic. He worked in the air force. My mom was a trader in the market. It was work buying and selling food and juice. My brother, Vo, is twenty-eight years old and still lives in Vietnam. Maybe, in the future, he will come here.

I'm from a family that likes food. My mom is a great cook. She cooks pho and moon cake; I like them very much. In Vietnam, my mom was a normal cook—not bad, not the best. But here, she's perfect because in America, not very many people can cook those foods.

In Vietnam, we lived with my grandma on a big farm with rice fields. The farm had many dogs and one cat. It was a big fat cat named Meo who only ate and slept. The dogs were Bin and Lu. The farm raised twenty pigs, ten cows, and three lines of chickens, with five chickens in one line.

Friends are a big motivation for me. In Vietnam, I had a best friend, Som. We were friends for eleven years. Here, I have an old friend from Vietnam named Hieu. We both live in America now. He helps me understand English and he translates for me. He is in college in California. I want to go to college like him, but not to the same school. I will go in Washington or New York. I came to America and made new friends. They are from all over the world. They help me have an easier future because I don't want a lonely life in the world. They are important to my identity and help me learn English.

Language is a big part of who I am. Learning languages helps me because other people can understand what I want. Vietnamese is my first language, but in Vietnamese, I can only talk with people in Vietnam. In English, I can talk to anybody, because English is the common language around the world.

The future is important to me. I will go to college because I want to learn everything. I have the opportunity to be a computer technician. In Vietnam, if you don't have money, you can't go to school. It wasn't fair to me, because I didn't have money. I can make a better future for myself in America, because America wants to help people.

Family, friends, language, and the future, are important to me. I want to finish school, get a good job, and have a simple life with my family and my girlfriend. I am happy because now I can live with my grandfather who came here years ago. I can make a better future for my family and me.

Mike Lawson lives in the Northwest and has published six politi-
cal thrillers: *The Inside Ring, The Second Perimeter, House Rules,*
House Secrets, House Justice, and *House Divided.* Two of his
novels have been nominated for the Barry Award. Prior to turning to writing full time, Mike was a nuclear engineer employed by
the United States Navy.

Canceled

MIKE LAWSON

WALTER DOOGAN LOOKED UP at the board and saw that his flight to Baltimore had been canceled. A month ago his flight to Cleveland had been canceled, and two months before that his flight to New York was delayed four hours and he missed an important meeting.

Walter decided that he'd had enough of this.

Walter had once been five feet nine inches tall; he was now an inch shorter in his sixth decade. He had worn glasses since the age of three, and his hair was intentionally full and long on the sides to hide his embarrassing, protruding ears. He was less embarrassed by his small pot belly. When people met him for the first time, they were always surprised such a remarkably accomplished man cut such an unimposing figure.

Walter walked up to the check-in counter and asked why the flight had been canceled. The man at the counter—too busy tapping a keyboard to even glance at him—muttered, "Weather in San Francisco."

Walter was prepared for this response. His flight to Baltimore was on a plane coming from San Francisco, and, before he approached the man, he had used his phone to check the weather in the Bay Area: sunny, seventy-two degrees, not a cloud in the sky, wind speed a gentle five miles per hour.

"The weather in San Francisco is perfect," Walter said. "I'd like to know why my flight was really canceled."

Now the man looked at him—and with the eyes of a fellow who knows he doesn't have to take crap from anybody. If Walter started throwing a tantrum, he would call security, and Walter would be dragged away, maybe arrested, possibly strip-searched, and his name would be put on a watch list.

"Look, Mister, I don't know why the flight was canceled. I was told weather. Now if you want to go to Baltimore, you need to go back to the main terminal and get in line and try to get on another flight."

"You mean," Walter innocently asked, "the airline isn't going to help me get on another flight?"

The man almost laughed and said, "Are you kidding me?" Instead he said, "No, sir, the airline is not required to help you get another flight if your flight is canceled due to weather. Look at the fine print on your ticket."

"And what about my luggage?" Walter said.

"Your luggage will be going to Baltimore on the next available flight. It'll get there before you do. Or maybe after you do. But it will get there eventually."

Walter nodded his head.

Yes, he'd had enough. He wasn't going to tolerate this any longer.

———

WALTER DOOGAN WAS one of the richest men in America. He started in real estate in Seattle, expanded into investment banking, and then launched into myriad other enterprises, all of which made him enormous amounts of money. But Walter didn't flaunt his wealth. His wife bought his clothes at Macy's, usually when the clothes were on sale; off-the-rack sizes fit him perfectly. He owned only two cars, both hybrids, because they were economical and green. He didn't own a yacht, because all the men he knew who owned yachts were so busy they hardly ever used them.

Walter certainly was too busy for a yacht. His home was modern and comfortable but only 2,500 square feet, because he and Mary didn't need a larger place now that the children were gone. And his home wasn't located in an exclusive, gated community like Broadmoor in Seattle, but instead in a working class neighborhood near Green Lake, because he and Mary liked to walk around the lake. He had thought often about buying his own jet—he could have afforded one easily—but had always rejected the idea. Why should he pay for a jet and a crew to fly it when there were dozens of airline companies that should be able to get him wherever he needed to go?

The problem with the airlines, Walter decided, was that no one who dealt with the customers ever felt responsible for anything. When your bags were lost, there was no one who could ever explain to you why they were lost or who had lost them. And they'd been lost at the airport you came from, not at the airport you were at, and the lost luggage folks weren't the least bit sympathetic—much less ashamed—that you'd be wearing the same clothes for the next two or three days.

If your flight was delayed, you had no idea why. Was it indeed weather-related, or was it because a pilot overslept or a mechanic failed to do routine maintenance on the plane? Or maybe the airline canceled the flight because it wasn't economical to fly a plane three-quarters full. And, of course, the airlines had no excess capacity to deal with an out-of-service plane because excess capacity negatively affected the bottom line—and the company cared more about the bottom line than it did about meeting its promise to its customers.

A promise. That's what Walter considered an airline ticket to be: a promise made to him by the airline to get him to a certain place at a certain time, but more and more these days they casually, callously, uncaringly broke that promise.

Walter sat down in one of the uncomfortable plastic chairs in the departure area and called the woman he was to have met that day in Baltimore.

He told her he wouldn't be able to attend the board meeting but that she could count on his company contributing $200,000 to the foundation, as previously committed. Promises meant something to Walter. He then used his phone to gather a few facts.

The airline that failed to get him to Baltimore paid its CEO—a man named Howard Getty—$4 million a year. And that didn't include Howard's bonus. The airline company itself had shown increasing profits three quarters in a row. At the same time, it had reduced salaries and benefits for its personnel, and health insurance premiums and pensions were now virtually the employees' total responsibility. And speaking of employees, there were 10 percent fewer of them than in the previous year, because the company had miraculously found a way to provide the same level of service without these people. It was no wonder, Walter thought, that airline company employees didn't really care.

Then he looked at the company's performance. He found a chart—the Internet was a marvelous thing—that showed the airline's on-time departure statistics for flights leaving from twenty major cities. The chart showed that the company's planes departed on schedule, on average, 85 percent of the time. Eighty-five percent! Can you imagine your car only starting 85 percent of the time? What if the Post Office lost 15 percent of your mail, or if you had electrical power in your home only twenty hours a day? Walter could not think of an entity, public or private, that performed so abysmally, and yet this particular airline was actually proud of its incompetence.

The other thing was that, when it came to airlines, the public's expectations had fallen so low that passengers passively accepted the situation. On a recent flight to Washington, D.C., Walter's plane was delayed for two hours in Seattle, and then the airline announced that people would be put on a different plane, but the plane would land at Reagan National instead of Dulles. Their baggage, however, would go to Dulles.

As Walter boarded the plane, he heard a woman say to her husband how lucky they were. Lucky! The woman actually felt grateful that she would arrive only two hours late and be landing at an airport that was thirty miles from her luggage. These days, if a plane was delayed for hours, folks felt lucky it hadn't been canceled. If their baggage showed up eight hours after they did, they felt lucky it hadn't been lost for good.

Walter was tired of these standards of "lucky."

—

WALTER GATHERED HIS TEAM about him in his office in downtown Seattle—an office with a magnificent view of Mount Rainier that Walter rarely noticed. His team consisted of twelve extremely bright young people he brought together whenever he launched a new endeavor. There was nothing these young folks couldn't do—and nothing they wouldn't do for Walter. He explained to them what he wanted, and they told him how it could be done. The fact that what Walter wanted was illegal didn't bother them; they knew he would protect them if they were caught and that he would certainly take the blame. Walter—all five feet eight inches of him—was, as they say, a stand-up guy.

The next morning, Walter called Mr. Howard Getty—Mr. Four-Million-Dollars-A-Year-Not-Counting-Bonuses Howard Getty. He told Mr. Getty that tomorrow morning, if his company's airplanes didn't leave Seattle on time, he'd be sorry. Mr. Getty responded by saying, "How did you get this number?" Followed by, "I'm calling Homeland Security and if . . . ." Walter hung up.

The next day, six of Mr. Getty's airplanes departed late—about what you'd expect from a company with an 85 percent on-time performance record—and by evening computers at Mr. Getty's corporate headquarters had the machine equivalent of a massive cerebral hemorrhage. The computers affected were not those that controlled flight schedules, however, but those that tracked investments and profits and dividends. Walter's young people said it would take Mr. Getty's accountants a month to recover from the meltdown.

The next day, Walter called Mr. Getty again, even though he'd been told there was a very good chance that the FBI would be listening in on the call. Walter told Mr. Getty that tomorrow, if all his airplanes didn't leave Seattle on time, he'd be sorry. Mr. Getty either didn't believe Walter or didn't have the ability to do anything useful, and four flights failed to depart on schedule.

Walter concluded the problem was that it wasn't personal for Mr. Getty. When Walter's young geniuses crashed the company's computers, Mr. Getty's company had been affected, his stockholders had been affected, but Mr. Getty wasn't really affected. His next attack on Mr. Getty had to be personal—just like it was personal for his customers when one of them missed a wedding or a funeral because Mr. Getty failed to perform. The following morning Mr. Getty was astounded to learn that $10,000 had been charged to his platinum credit card to buy sporting equipment for an inner city youth program.

One of Walter's young people informed him that, this time, Mr. Getty finally did do something to improve things: He diverted two extra aircraft to Seattle to deal with unexpected delays and sent a strongly worded email to various executives stating that heads would roll if every plane didn't leave Seattle on time. So when Walter called Mr. Getty again, he said that tomorrow, if every plane didn't leave Portland, Oregon, on time, he'd be sorry. Walter felt good about helping Seattle's neighbor to the south. "Furthermore," Walter said, "no lost luggage, Mr. Getty." Since airline companies lose about 14,000 bags a day, according to one report Walter read, he figured Mr. Getty should be very motivated.

The next day, seven flights failed to depart Portland on time—it appeared that one of the extra planes diverted to Seattle had come from Portland—and twenty-two passengers arrived in Detroit without their luggage, as did sixteen deplaning in Minneapolis. Mrs. Getty was mortified when she couldn't pay for lunch at the Chicago Ritz-Carleton because all her credit cards had been canceled. Mr. Getty's daughter at Yale suffered a similar embarrassment when she tried to buy a new pair of $300 hole-in-the knees jeans. But the real ruckus was raised by Mr. Getty's board of directors—the people who could fire Mr. Getty if they were so inclined. They were extremely upset to discover that they, just like Mr. Getty, had been very generous to a number of Walter's favorite charities.

Mr. Getty was also annoyed that the FBI agents responsible for protecting his airline from a madman were rather blasé about the whole situation. The agents had originally feared some sort of terrorist plot, but the only ones being terrorized were a bunch of rich folks who usually flew on corporate jets. What Mr. Getty didn't appreciate was that every agent assigned to the case had personally and frequently experienced the ineptitude of airline companies, and, although they were doing their best to catch the culprit, their hearts weren't really in the game. The media, of course, became aware of what Walter was doing—they became aware because Walter had called them—and the overwhelming response from the public was that whoever was secretly attacking Mr. Getty was their hero, an honest-to-God, real-life Batman.

The following day, Walter called Mr. Getty again. Walter's young people had him make the call from a moving vehicle, and he was told that his voice was being bounced off a Russian satellite. Walter didn't really care.

"Hello," Walter said.

"What do you want from me?" Mr. Getty said. "Just tell me what you want."

"I want you to do your job, Mr. Getty. Now I've checked the weather and tomorrow, all across these United States, there's nary a storm predicted. It's going to be a glorious day. Therefore, I expect all your planes to depart on time tomorrow and ...."

"That's impossible!" Mr. Getty screamed.

"Well, it shouldn't be," Walter said. "You've promised all the people you sold tickets to that your planes would leave on time. If you know that's not possible, you shouldn't schedule your planes the way you do. And no lost luggage, Mr. Getty."

Mr. Getty's board of directors was outraged when 138 planes failed to depart on time. They'd never been outraged by such poor performance in the past, but this time things were different because their credit cards no longer worked, nor did their cell phones or laptops. Security alarms were going off at their homes and condos, and their PIN numbers wouldn't silence the alarms. They became apoplectic when they couldn't get cash from ATM machines. The final straw may have been when they discovered their credit ratings were now comparable to those of single, working mothers and recent college graduates.

Mr. Getty was fired the following day.

———

WALTER DOOGAN STEPPED OUT of the airport shuttle and tipped the driver 15 percent. He always took the shuttle to the airport, because it only cost $18, and the shuttle had never been late getting him to his plane. It was a good company, and Walter was happy to give them his business.

He checked his baggage at the curb, verifying that the tags showed his suitcase was indeed going to Phoenix. He checked the departure board when he entered the terminal, and it showed that his flight was expected to depart on time. Nonetheless, he really didn't want to be late arriving in Phoenix; his favorite niece was graduating from high school that evening. He took out his cell phone—a new one his young people had given him—and made a phone call to Mr. Getty's replacement.

Author's Note: The on-time performance, lost luggage, and CEO salary data given in this story is for a real airline, and the story about the flight being diverted from Dulles to Reagan National actually happened to my wife and me. My wife said to me, "Quit complaining! We're just lucky we're getting to D.C. today." I can't tell you how much I wished that Walter Doogan existed.

Photo by Fat Yeti Photography.

Elizabeth Austen is the author of the poetry collection *Every Dress a Decision* (Blue Begonia Press, 2011) and two chapbooks, *The Girl Who Goes Alone* (Floating Bridge Press, 2010) and *Where Currents Meet* (one of four winners of the 2010 Toadlily Press chapbook award and part of the quartet Sightline). She produces poetry-related programming for the Seattle NPR affiliate KUOW 94.9.

The Girl Who Goes Alone

ELIZABETH AUSTEN

Here's the thing about being a girl
and wanting to play outside.
All the grown-ups grind it into you from the get go:
girls outside aren't safe.
The guy in the car? If he rolls down the window and leans his head out,
     run
because the best you can hope for is a catcall, and at worst
you'll wind up with your face on the side of a milk carton.

Even when you're a grown-up girl, your father—because he loves you—
will send you a four-page article about how to protect yourself
while standing at the ATM, while traveling unescorted, while jogging
     solo,
an article informing you how to distinguish phony police
and avoid purse snatchers, pickpockets, rapists, and thugs.

Tell someone you're going into the woods alone
and they'll story your head with trailside cougar attacks,

cave dwelling misogynists, lightning strikes, forest fires, flash floods,
and psychopaths with a sixth sense for a woman alone in a tent.

To be a girl alone in the wilderness is to know
that if something goes wrong—
you picked the trailhead where the ax murderer lurks
or the valley of girl-eating gophers—
if you don't come home intact, the mourning
will be mixed with I-told-you-sos
from everyone whose idea of camping involves an RV or a Motel 6.
The message is clear: Girls must be chaperoned.

So, when, at the end of the day, you zip up the tent
and lie back in your sleeping bag,
fleece jacket bundled into a lumpy pillow under your head,
the second you close your eyes every least night noise
 is instantly magnified.

—

You lie there and consider the pungent heft of menstrual blood,
how even your sweat is muskier, louder, when you're bleeding.
Not hard to imagine its animal allure—every bear
for miles around sniffing you on the night wind.

You lie there, listening, running a mental inventory of any
potentially scented item—

did every one make it into the food bag hung from a tree?
Toothpaste, trail mix, ChapStick, sunscreen—crap.
Sunscreen still in your pack, nestled right beside you
where Outdoor Man used to sleep. So you're up, out of the tent
headlamp casting its too-bright spotlight, darkening the dark outside
     its reach
as you lower the bag, shove the sunscreen in, hoist and tie.

Far enough from the ground to elude the bears?
Far enough along the branch to thwart raccoons?
Tree far enough from the tent to keep from signaling
the proximity of ground-level, girl-shaped snacks?

You go alone—in part—to prove that though Outdoor Man has left you
his body is the only geography he can deprive you of.
He can give his muscled calves and thighs, his shoulders, chest,
     and hands
to another woman, but not the Sauk River old growth,
snow fields of Rainier, sea stacks of Shi Shi.

He can keep you from the sweet, blood-thrilling hum
of his body, but not the sweaty, blood-thumping
pleasure of a hard-earned panoramic view or high-altitude starlight.

The thing about being a girl who goes alone, who goes
again and again, is that it freaks
the potential next boyfriend. He doesn't want
to be out machoed and he doesn't want to admit it
and he hopes you can't tell. The thing about being the girl who still
     goes alone is that it proves

you don't need him and no matter how you show him you want him
it's not the same
and you both know it.

———

Zipped back into the tent you remind yourself you've never
 really been in danger.
When have you ever been in danger? Well there was that boy,
     but years ago
a teenager like you, driving around bored and pissed
at the world, his BB gun and his father's two rifles
on the seat beside him. Lucky you.
The gun he leveled on the window ledge
lodged nothing more than a BB in your thigh.

The thing about being a girl alone in the woods is
 you know too much
about the grain of truth in the warnings.

Even if you seem impervious, weird good luck leaving you
     so far unscathed
you know the other girls' stories—your sister
date raped after a party in college, a friend
raped by a stranger at knifepoint, the two women
shot on the Pinnacle Lake trail, the singer
killed by coyotes in Nova Scotia.

The thing
about being a girl
who goes alone
is that you feel like you shouldn't go
if you're afraid. If you go it should mean you're not afraid,
that you're never afraid. Your friends will think that you go
 unafraid.

This girl
who goes alone
is always afraid, always negotiating to keep the voices
in her head at a manageable pitch of hysteria.

I go knowing that there will be a moment—maybe long moments, maybe
hours of them, maybe the whole trip—
when I curse myself for going alone.
When I lie in the tent and all I am is fear.

———

I walk into the wilderness alone
because the animal in me needs to fill her nose
 with the scent of stone and lichen,
ocean salt and pine forest warming in early sun.

I walk in the wilderness alone so I can hear myself.
So I can feel real to myself.

I go because I know I'm lucky to have a car, gas money, days off
the back and legs and appetite
to take me there.
I go while I still can.

The girl who goes alone
claims for herself
the madrone juniper daybreak.

She claims hemlock prairie falcon nightfall
nurse log sea star glacial moraine
huckleberry trillium salal
snowmelt avalanche lily waterfall
birdsong limestone granite moonlight schist
cirque saddle summit ocean
she claims the curve of the earth.

The girl who goes alone says with her body
the world is worth the risk.

The Girl Who Goes Alone *was commissioned for the 2009 Literary Series at Richard Hugo House.*

PHOTO NOT AVAILABLE.

Estefani is nineteen years old and from Mexico. She loves soccer and reading. In the future, she will be an interpreter.

My Change: My Life in Mexico and America

ESTEFANI

I am from Mexico, the country,
And Puebla, the city.
I came to the United States
To learn more English and to know a different life.

I am from Tecina 36 Secondary School.
My school was beautiful and big.
Green, white, and red, like the colors of my flag.
Pine trees outside,
Pink, orange, red, and yellow roses.
It had a small cafeteria and a big garden.
All the students wore uniforms.
I wore a brown skirt, maroon sweater,
White shirt, black shoes,
And white knee socks.

I am from the market Hidalgo.
From tamales with big tortillas and chicken or pork.

From atole made with milk and chocolate or strawberries.
From mole—spicy, chocolate, the most typical food of Puebla.
From camote sweets and ponche—
Iced tea with apples, guava, peaches, and pineapple.

I am from my warm family.
Not big, not small.
From Puebla, Mexico.
There are seven of us:
My sisters, Nahomy and Liliana,
My brothers, Luis and Israel,
My dad, my mom, and me.
In Mexico, we are united.
All my family—*estamos unidos.*

In America—*Los Estados Unidos,*
It's only my daughter, Viridiana, and me,
My brother, Israel, and
My cousins, Armondo and Viridiana.

In Mexico, I was the daughter.
Here, I am the mother.

I will teach to my daughter
The new ideas that I learn.

A new country, new customs, and a new life.

Sam Howe Verhovek has been reading—and writing—in the rain since 1998, the year he moved to Seattle to become the Pacific Northwest correspondent for *The New York Times*. A Boston native, he lives in Magnolia with his wife, Lisa, and their three children, Gordie, Alice, and Johnny. Favorite Rain City factoid: the Seattle Metropolitans won the Stanley Cup in 1917, and Seattle became the first American city to do so. Look it up! Sam is currently at work on a book about baseball in the Dominican Republic during the Trujillo era.

Jet City

SAM HOWE VERHOVEK

IN THE SEATTLE OF 1955, there was no Space Needle yet, no iconic, futuristic structure to give the city a signature skyline. Tucked away in that quiet upper-left-hand corner of the map, Seattle was still seven years away from hosting the World's Fair, and twelve years from gaining its first major-league sports team. Yet Seattle had something to show the world, and in recent months the eye and ear had been drawn upward toward it—a large, loud fast-moving blur of metal soaring over the waters of Puget Sound and above the Cascade and Olympic mountain ranges. This 95-ton silver, brown, and canary yellow-colored bird was the prototype for a passenger jet being developed by the local aircraft company. That firm happened to have been located in Seattle nearly forty years before on the whim of a young Michigan lumber and mining magnate and Ivy League dropout.

William Edward Boeing—his German father was named Wilhelm Böing, the son wound up with an Anglicized version of the name, and told most everyone to call him Bill—had come to the Pacific Northwest just after the turn of the century to check out the timber prospects. They were fine, indeed, and Bill Boeing settled in Hoquiam, a tough little logging town near the Pacific coast in southwestern Washington State.

This wealthy, strapping, and energetic young man became much wealthier, buying and selling timber tracts, and before too long he was spending most of his time in Seattle, itself a somewhat rough-around-the-edges port town, but a decidedly more upscale place than Hoquiam. And when his fancy was seized by flight during his very first trip aloft, aboard a hydroplane over Seattle's Lake Washington on the Fourth of July in 1914, it did not take long for Bill Boeing to imagine himself as an aircraft maker. He respected the skills of the pilot, Terah Maroney, but he did not think so highly of the pilot's boxy, drafty, stick-and-wire Curtis floatplane, he told a friend who also flew that day, G. Conrad Westervelt, a naval lieutenant and engineer. Then Bill Boeing made a rather brass assertion.

"You know, Westervelt," he said, "there isn't much to that machine of Maroney's. I think we could build a better one!"

The Boeing & Westervelt B & W Seaplane, made of wood, wire, and Irish linen, with a 125-horsepower engine and a top speed of 75 miles per hour, was in the air by June 1916. Westervelt was called back East for naval duty, and soon the company was all Boeing's. Though the market for airplanes was much larger on the other side of the country, Boeing decided to stick it out in Seattle chiefly for this reason: there was so much good *wood* in the area. "Built Where the Spruce Grows" was the Boeing Airplane Company's motto. As time went by, aluminum replaced wood as the preferred material for aircraft, and as it happened, the Pacific Northwest was an ideal place for this commodity, too. Cheap hydropower from the Columbia and other great rivers of the region powered the plants that produced all the aluminum. The phenomenal efforts of Boeing and other aircraft manufacturers helped lead the Allies to victory in World War II. But as the 1950s dawned and the Korean War sputtered down into a standoff, the Boeing Airplane Company had a giant challenge on its hands, one that company executives sometimes delicately referred to as "the peace problem." While Boeing had thrived as a military manufacturer, its performance in the commercial market bordered on the anemic. It suffered from something of a Goldilocks syndrome: some of its civilian planes wound up too small for the passenger market, and some too big.

In 1933, the Boeing company had introduced what, at that time, was a stunningly modern airplane, the 160-mile-per-hour, ten-passenger, twin-engine Boeing 247, the first airliner with all-metal construction, deicing equipment, and retractable landing gear. It had a ceiling just under six feet high.

But Boeing's innovative airliner quickly turned into an also-ran to a legendary airplane built by the Southern California–based Douglas Aircraft Company. The Douglas engineers had countered the 247 with the fourteen-passenger DC-2, soon followed by the twenty-one-passenger DC-3. The DC-3 (along with its military counterpart, the C-47) was one of the most successful airplanes ever built, more than thirteen thousand in all, flown by airlines all over the world and even in use today, for everything from all-cargo trips around Alaska to aid missions in Africa. In 1939, a single model of airplane, the DC-3, carried 90 percent of the world's airline passengers.

Powered by two large propeller engines, the DC-3 had two large tires under the front of its fuselage and a single, smaller one in back. It was ungainly but strangely compelling in takeoff. As the DC-3 lumbered down a runway, it tilted upward in such a way that it was abruptly rolling on its front wheels, looking for all the world like it might tip over on its snout. With a bit more speed, however improbably, it jumped off the runway and headed for the clouds.

Douglas Aircraft seemed to have a magic touch as it developed new, bigger, propeller planes into the 1950s: the DC-4, the DC-6, the DC-7 (nicknamed "the Seven Seas"). However bumpy the ride or how many refueling stops needed to get there, these were the planes used by most of the world's carriers to get their passengers across the country or across the oceans.

Meanwhile, Lockheed Aircraft was working in concert with Trans World Airlines' principal owner, Howard Hughes, who even with spells of madness was one of the most visionary figures in aviation history. Together they came up with the elegant Lockheed Constellation, nicknamed the Connie, a dolphin-shaped, triple-tailed, four-engine airplane that in some configurations was the most luxurious machine ever to soar in the sky. Some had eighteen sleeper cabins, with crisp-linen sheets, turndown service, fresh flowers, and four-course meals.

Boeing, by contrast, was a three-time loser in the commercial aviation industry. Not only was the 247 a slow seller, but the company also lost millions on the big, bulbous-nosed Flying Clipper airships operated by Pan American World Airways in the late 1930s, and it lagged with the luxurious but expensive "Stratocruiser," a giant flying tub of a plane that was vastly outsold by its Douglas and Lockheed competitors.

As the 1950s began, Seattle-based Boeing had less than 1 percent of the existing commercial aircraft market, and even that share was eroding, for Boeing did not even have a single new commercial airliner in the design stage. But in a way, Boeing's failures contained promising seeds of fortune— for the company made a move initially eschewed by its more successful competitors in civil aviation. Boeing decided to build a jet airliner.

Boeing's decision represented an astounding gamble and, for five lonely years, the company forged ahead without even persuading a *single customer* to commit to buying its airplane, in either its commercial or military configurations. Some of the best and brightest luminaries in the airline industry questioned whether there was much need or demand for jet-speed travel. "We can't go backward to the jet," said C.R. Smith, president of American Airlines, announcing a large order for more of the prop-driven DC-7s that were already raking in plenty of money for both Douglas and America. Ralph Damon, president of Trans World Airlines, said simple economics favored a $1.5 million propliner such as the Constellation over the

$4 million jet being peddled by Boeing, even if the latter offered a faster and less bumpy ride to the passenger. "The only thing wrong with the jet planes of today," said the head of TWA, "is that they won't make any money."

So Boeing built a single prototype, officially called the 367-80 but much more widely known by the company nickname Dash-80, and this was the plane that had started showing up in the skies over the Puget Sound region in 1954.

The airplane would become known as the 707, a machine whose DNA can be deduced in any Boeing jetliner designed and flown since. It was perhaps not as recklessly beautiful as the British de Havilland Comet, the world's very first jet airliner. Rather than sleekly hiding the engines by building them into the wing roots, the Dash-80's jets hung down somewhat ungainly from the wings on spindly struts. This was a more practical if less

© The Boeing Company Collection at The Museum of Flight

The Dash-80 on a flight around Mt. Rainier.

elegant placement, allowing easier maintenance and even a quick replacement if needed. It would prove safer. The windows were rounded—not as crisp as the straight lines that made up the squared windows on the Comet, whose designers wanted them that way to distinguish their airplane's windows from the porthole windows of a ship. That insistence would prove costly, in so many ways.

More than anything, though, the Dash-80 was big. In fact, it could hold nearly three times as many passengers as the original Comet, and even the company's top officials conceded the plane was so much bigger than any before it that a single crash could instantly become the most deadly accident in the history of aviation, perhaps even the death knell for the whole enterprise. "It was a question of policy as to whether you should expose one hundred people to the hazards of commercial aviation, and whether Boeing could survive the headlines of a hundred people being killed in a single crash," recalled one senior executive, Maynard Pennell.

Moreover, Boeing, after fishing around with zero success among the nation's major airlines to find a paying partner in the development of its jetliner, took an audacious step when it decided to build the plane on its own. The board committed $15 million—a huge figure for the day, representing a quarter of the firm's net worth—for research and development of what it simply called "Project X." It did so largely at the prodding of one man: William McPherson Allen, the company president.

Self-effacing, introspective, a balding, jug-eared lawyer raised in small-town Montana, Allen hardly fit the mold of a swashbuckling gambler. The airline world was full of such larger-than-life characters—Trippe of Pan Am; Hughes of TWA; Rickenbacker of Eastern, which dominated lucrative routes linking the Northeast with Florida vacation spots and the rest of the South.

Bill Allen was not a pilot. He was not an engineer. He recalled no childlike fascination with flight—and, in any event, airplanes were certainly not a major sight in the Big Sky country in the early 1900s, when he was growing up in the Bitterroot Valley community of Lolo. He was conservative by nature, in his politics and, at first, with his approach to Boeing's finances. But Bill Allen, in his own quiet way, wound up as the biggest gambler of all. Twice he would push the Boeing board of directors to bet the company on a single commercial airplane—the 707 in the early 1950s and the 747 in the late 1960s—a financing and development strain that could easily push it to the brink of bankruptcy.

It was Bill Allen who sat on a boat this sunny August day in 1955 with old friends, relaxing and awaiting the start of Seattle's famed hydroplane Gold Cup races on Lake Washington. He was one of three hundred fifty thousand people gathered in or around the lake to watch the races, and among the crowd were hundreds of visitors who made up a veritable who's who of the world's aviation industry. For at this time, Seattle was the host to two major conventions—that of the International Air Transport Association, or IATA, a sort of mini-United Nations organization that regulated routes and fares of the world's international airlines, and of the American Institute of Aeronautics, which represented the nation's leading aviation engineers.

Word was leaked that Boeing's Dash-80 jet would do a test run during a break in the race schedule. For many in the air industry, it would be their very first look at the giant jet plane. There was still much skepticism about the economics of a jet—and concern about whether it was safe.

The massive bird lumbered down the runway, south of downtown Seattle, and headed west out over the Olympic Peninsula for an initial round of tests. This was an airplane insured for $18 million, with one unusual provision in the contract. Only one man could be at the controls.

This man was Alvin M. "Tex" Johnston, the company's chief test pilot, who oozed all of the swagger that Allen, his boss, kept so carefully in check. Strong, profane, and funny, he was a character practically out of Hollywood's central casting—in fact, he would one day serve as a model for the Slim Pickens bomber-pilot character in Stanley Kubrick's dark-comedy

Cold War classic, *Dr. Strangelove*. Johnston often insisted on wearing his cowboy boots and even his Stetson when he flew, and on the wall of his office at Boeing headquarters he hung a sign that, however humorously, let people know his view of his place in the pecking order of a company filled with brilliant designers and engineers.

"One test is worth a thousand expert opinions," the sign read.

Everybody called him Tex, though few knew the gag behind the name: he was actually from Kansas, and he'd acquired the nickname one day early in his career in Niagara Falls, New York, where he was testing fighter planes. Arriving at work one day in 1943 in his trademark Stetson and polished cowboy boots, Johnston got an approving nod from a mechanic, who said: "Get your 'chute, Tex. You get the first one today." The name stuck.

Boeing President Bill Allen speaks with chief test pilot Tex Johnston.

Johnston got his start as a barnstormer in his native state, where at one point he earned his keep as a daredevil with Inman's Flying Circus, for which he played the part of a drunken country bumpkin, flying crazy loops and zags with his Ford trimotor plane as nervous audiences craned their necks to watch the show and see whether he'd crash. Occasionally he'd do a complete roll of the airplane.

At Boeing, the chief pilot irritated the engineers by cussing if he didn't like their drawings. He was a font of corny sayings: nobody died, in Tex Johnston's world, he just "departed from the earth-bound flight pattern." And he could be crude. The Tex Johnston of this era wouldn't make it through the first three minutes of today's workplace-sensitivity training.

In a psychoanalyst's office in 1948 in Seattle's Capitol Hill neighborhood, Tex Johnston was undergoing a mandatory preemployment mental-fitness evaluation. The female doctor interviewing him was tall, with "liquid brown eyes," complemented by "dark brunette hair and her full and enticing mouth," as Johnston cheerfully described it all a half century or so later. He said he "played along" when she pulled out the standard peg set of the era, and complied by putting the round pegs in the round holes and the square pegs in the square holes. Then she asked a series of questions—Why are you a test pilot? Why did you choose Boeing?—winding up at: "What do you like better than anything in the world?"

"Copulation!" said Tex.

The interview was over. Apparently he passed, since Boeing hired him, though he was rejected when he asked the analyst for a date. "I'm new in Seattle, but I understand the Ben Franklin has a delightful restaurant, the Outrigger," said Tex as he stood up to leave. "Would you have dinner with me tonight?" The woman stared at him for a moment. "No-o-o," she drew out her answer. "I believe not." Johnston walked out with a tip of his cowboy hat, and said: "It was indeed a pleasure."

Tex Johnston's actual engineering instruction in the principles of aero-dynamics was limited, but he was nonetheless recognized as a genius at fly-ing, a sort of Michael Jordan among pilots, a man with a sixth—and seventh, and eighth—sense of what his airplane could do.

Tex, an admiring colleague once said, "could make anything fly."

Johnston was cruising on this Sunday afternoon at about 450 miles per hour in the Dash-80 when he cut it back and came down over Lake Washington at only 300 feet. The audience ooh'd and aah'd and pointed at the brightly colored jet. He pulled the big jet up at a 35-degree climb. And then the screaming plane dipped its wing and started to turn over, rotating slowly, at one point completely upside down, the yellow-and-silver tail sec-tion pointing straight down toward the water and the jet's huge underbelly facing upward toward the heavens.

On board his boat, Allen, the company president, briefly felt sick to his stomach. The 707 was his baby, and it looked to be soaring out of control. If it crashed anywhere near the crowd, it could cause hundreds of deaths. If it crashed anywhere, the 707 project would clearly be dead—and so would the company.

But then, as Allen and the rest of the crowd watched, the plane con-tinued its roll until it had completed a full 360-degree rotation. The plane soared several hundred feet higher, then reversed course and came in again toward the lake—toward all the boats in the water, toward the huge crowds on shore.

Again, the Boeing 707 prototype tilted and went into a slow, full-circle rotation overhead. No one could hear Tex Johnston, of course, but up in the pilot's seat, he was letting out whoops of joy.

This time, Bill Allen did not feel sick. He managed to stammer out a joke to Larry Bell of Bell Aircraft, one of his guests on the boat. "Larry, give me about ten of those heart pills you've been taking," he said. "I need 'em worse than you do."

Rollout of the "Dash-80," the prototype for the Boeing 707.

Inside, though, Bill Allen was no longer worried. Now, he was seething. As soon as the boat got to shore, he called a meeting of his top executives for early the next morning at Boeing headquarters, and there was only one item on the agenda: what to do with Boeing's chief test pilot, Tex Johnston.

Excerpted from Jet Age: The Comet, the 707, and the Race to Shrink the World *by Sam Howe Verhovek, by arrangement with Avery, a member of Penguin Group (USA) Inc., Copyright © 2010.*

Northwest Field Recording—WA (7 inch/B side), Victoria Haven, 2010

Seattle Art Museum, Gift of Rebecca and Alexander Stewart and an anonymous donor, 2011.9.1. © Victoria Haven

2

UNSTOPPABLE FORCES

Photo by Frank Huster.

Garth Stein is the author of three novels, including the *New York Times* and international bestseller, *The Art of Racing in the Rain*. He has also worked as a playwright and documentary filmmaker, and is the co-founder of Seattle7Writers, a literary non-profit organization.

The Peculiar Intelligence of Parrots

GARTH STEIN

HAVE YOU BOLTED your house to its foundation yet?

I mean, look at the maps. Read the reports. "The Cascadia Subduction Zone is due for a 9.0 magnitude quake within the next fifty years." "A catastrophic quake resulting in liquefaction of soil." "Sheer damage will be extreme, resulting in severing of communications, electric, gas, water, and all other utilities."

Liquefaction. You know what that means. The ground on which you are standing turns into something similar to water. Not cool.

I repeat: Have you bolted your house to its foundation yet?

Yeah, neither have my parents. They haven't stocked three days worth of water, either. Three gallons per person per day. They haven't packed a suitcase with extra clothes, set aside a flashlight and batteries, bought a battery- operated radio, stockpiled any cash, topped off their gas tanks.

I repeat: Have you bolted your?... Forget it. You never listen.

MY DAD HAD this line he thought was really funny. If he and my mom were fighting—not an unusual occurrence—he would say, "Every other weekend, two weeks over the summer, and Christmases in odd numbered years." He would pause, and then deliver his punch line: "Those are the times you can come stay with me in my condo in West Seattle when the divorce is finalized."

It was a joke, of course. He was making light of their fighting, and by doing so, he felt he was diffusing my apprehension about the state of their miserable relationship. Like, "we might be fighting, but we will never get divorced because we love each other so much." That's funny, right? Ha! But then one weekend I found myself sitting in my divorced dad's condo in West Seattle, and I realized that sometimes when people make jokes, they're actually foretelling the future. Like Cassandra, who I learned about in the mythology unit we did in school. She could tell the future, but no one would believe her. Imagine you could tell the future, but you didn't even believe yourself. That's my dad. The shape of an "L" on his forehead.

MY NAME IS TREVOR and I live in Seattle near Seward Park, and I'm in the sixth grade. I have a little brother who's kind of cool. His name is Joseph Benjamin, so we call him Joby. He's only five. Which means my parents didn't have sex very often. Like once every seven years or so. Which is part of the reason that my dad is living in West Seattle and my mom is dating her Pilates instructor.

I'm pretty much in charge of Joby, because my mother isn't really good at the whole "mother thing." Her words. So I've become a really good cook. Frozen waffles. Pop Tarts. Hot dogs. Basically, anything you can shove into a toaster oven or microwave.

So one afternoon, when all the responsible adults were away, I put a couple of frozen burritos in the micro for Joby and me, and I turned on the TV—local news so I could check the weather—and there was a feature item about a whole bunch of parrots living in Seward Park. For real. Wild parrots. They'd escaped, or they'd been liberated or something. A huge gang of feral parrots living in Seward Park, maybe 200 of them and they're really smart.

Scientists figured people just let them go because parrots squawk a lot, so people probably get sick of them and set them free. Not a big market for secondhand parrots on Craigslist. So when the burritos were ready, I wrapped them in paper towels, put Joby in his Chariot, and took him down there to look for them.

Seward Park has some of the last old growth forest in the whole world, so it's sort of a deep, rich forest with a ton of poison oak—or at least a ton of poison oak signs—which keeps people away and makes it a safe haven for feral parrots.

Joby and I went up the hill and into the woods, and the city faded away. Except for airplanes, we couldn't hear anything man-made. Not even the I-90 bridge. Joby saw the first one. It looked like a dirty bird from a distance. Dark and scruffy with a long tail. But it had a distinctive curved beak, and a round head and upright stance, and when I looked at it I was mesmerized. A parrot in Seward Park.

I looked around and realized the trees were full of them. Old gray parrots. I shouldn't say that. They might not have been old, but they were definitely gray. That comes from malnutrition, apparently.

"Polly want a cracker?" I asked, and I took out a box of Ritz crackers and tossed one of them high into the air. None of them budged. Not even a blink. I tried again. Nothing.

"Polly want a peanut?" I asked, and this time I fired a whole roasted, unsalted peanut at one parrot's head, and I swear to God, that parrot reached out with its foot and snatched the peanut out of the sky, looked at it, cracked it open with its sharp beak, and ate the nuts right out of it. Then he looked at me—right at me—wondering if I might have more.

I had more. I fired another peanut at the same parrot and got the same result. And soon, Joby and I were covered with parrots.

I THINK IT WAS GOOD that my parents got divorced, because they didn't like each other. But I also think it wasn't so good, because they didn't like themselves, either. At least when they were together, they had something in common. When they broke up, they became lonely and self-destructive. But who am I to judge?

Joby and I looked after each other that summer, since my mom was either working or with Jake, the Pilates instructor, and my dad was either working or roller blading down to Alki Point so he could look at the girls. So Joby and I started spending a lot of time with the parrots. They got to know us pretty quickly, and seemed to be expecting us whenever we arrived. We figured them out, too. Which ones were the peanut freaks, which preferred no-salt baldy pretzels, and which liked Goldfish crackers. They all liked raisins and dried mangos.

After we started having lunch with them every day, we noticed that color started coming back into their feathers, so maybe we were doing something good for the universe. In any event, we went to Seward Park every day that summer, except the weekends we spent in West Seattle with my dad, and on those days, we felt really bad about not feeding our friends. Honestly, we grew pretty attached to them; they were the most dependable family we'd ever had.

PARROTS DON'T TALK, they imitate. They can sound like they're talking, but they don't really form sentences. They're like Xerox machines made out of feathers and blood.

But, apparently, they read.

And one day, when Joby and I went to visit our friends for lunch, they brought a whole bunch of newspapers for us to see, which I didn't think was totally weird, at first. They collected them, I figured. I mean they live in a busy park in the middle of the city. People leave their papers around, the parrots steal them, whatever. And I might have thought it was random, the papers they brought us that day. Except they were all from different months and even different years. And they all featured one of three things: a story about earthquake probability, a story about hot air balloons, or advertisements for rubber rafts.

"What do you think?" I asked Joby as we studied the papers, though Joby just looked at the pictures since he couldn't read.

He said: "An earthquake's coming; they want us to get ready."

I love Joby. Five years old and he plays the piano like a crazy sick piano genius. I'm serious. Not like a little kid who's been taking lessons for years and can play some Chopin Etude that's been pounded into his head by a $40-an-hour piano teacher. Joby, who has never taken a piano lesson in his life, can hear a song on the radio and then sit at an empty piano at a shopping mall or school auditorium or some friend's house where my mother has dumped us for a weekend so she could go to an ashram with her boyfriend because my dad refused to take us because "it wasn't on his schedule." Joby can sit down and play that song. Beautifully. Straight out of his head. Like—bang! He can freaking play some freaking Elton John song or Billy Joel. And, sure, it's corny like, *New York State of Mind*. But he can play it so good, it makes you cry. I swear to God. *That's* what pisses me off about all this. Joby should be famous. He should be on *America's Got Talent*, or something. He shouldn't be lost to anonymity and mediocrity because his parents are losers. (Did I tell you about the "L" on my *mother's* forehead? It's bigger than my father's.)

Look, I'm busy. I'm in sixth grade. I've got tons of work to do all the time. And my parents are screw-ups. So while I was impressed by the newspaper collection presented to me by the feral parrots of Seward Park, and while I was moved by my bother's assessment of those articles, I guess, like any adult figure, I ignored the signs.

It was a few weeks after the newspaper incident that the next strange thing happened. My dad was bringing us home from West Seattle one morning, and he stopped abruptly in the middle of Thirty-first Avenue.

A family of five raccoons was crossing the street. Not panicked, not rushing. Just trotting across the wide street.

"I've never seen raccoons in the day before," I said to my dad.

"Neither have I," he admitted. "They're probably rabid. Stay away from them."

But they didn't look rabid.

And then, that night Jake, the Pilates instructor, told me to take out the compost, so I hauled the stinky bag up the stairs to the compost bin in the back alley, and I saw a coyote run by. Really! A coyote! What are the odds? Seward Park. Raccoons. Coyotes. Parrots bringing newspapers.

I'm no genius. But I'm not a dumb ass, either. I got myself ready.

A BLOW-UP RAFT and foot pump. Two hundred feet of nylon rope cut into five-foot lengths. Lightweight extendable paddle. Five bags of roasted, unsalted peanuts. Seventy-nine dollars of accumulated cash gifts, excluding coins (too heavy). My dad's FireWand grill lighter. A survival radio my Uncle Lester gave me before he vanished mysteriously (possibly a Jewish mafia kill, my dad says). Water purification tablets I got with my mom's REI dividend, because she never uses it. Water bottles for me and Joby. Jalapeño beef jerky I shoplifted from Leschi Market because it's so good, but I always felt guilty about it, so I never ate it. Underwear and socks for me and Joby.

That's what's in my earthquake preparedness kit. What's in yours?

MY MOTHER WAS over at Jake's house when it started. She said I was big enough to watch Joby, and I should call her if anything went wrong. Jake lived on Beacon Hill so she wasn't far away, and probably nothing serious would happen and don't answer the door and don't answer the phone, but if I needed anything, call her and she'd be over in a minute....

If you've never been in one, let me tell you: it's scarier than you could even imagine. It starts as sort of a rumble, a deep ocean wave, but the ground is the ocean. And the dogs start barking right away, and then the car alarms go off, and it's like a cacophony of sound. But when the shaking doesn't stop right away and grows into an earth dance, and when you can picture these tectonic plates, huge, massive in scale, ramming against each other twenty miles below the ground, you realize how tiny you are compared to what's happening. Just like in mythology, titans are clashing. And you. You are a speck on a speck of one of their swords.

When the electricity goes out, and the dogs are so afraid they've stopped howling, but the wave is still going, even though you've counted to twenty a bunch of times—that's when it gets really scary. When it keeps going beyond that.

THE FIRST THING I do is make sure I'm alive, and I am. So the next thing I do is make sure Joby is alive, and he is. And that's very good.

Our entire house—not bolted to the foundation, by the way—has slid down the hill and is resting neatly in the street. It is night. There is no power. Car alarms are going off everywhere. There are no sirens; I picture all the ambulances, police cars, and fire trucks buried in rubble. There are only car alarms. That's a comfort. When I become the new President of the Universe, I will have all car alarm designers put to death.

Joby is pretty good on his bicycle, but I don't know what we'll encounter on our journey, so I hook his Chariot up to my bike and pile it full with our survival stuff, and I wheel us out to the street.

The world is full of people in pajamas. They're all standing outside their houses—or what is left of their houses; many are in rubble. They're scratching their bleeding heads. Some of them are screaming in pain. But the ones who are not in pain, are silent, like zombies. Silent, staring witnesses to absolute and total destruction. Mount Baker Park is a hole in the ground, maybe fifty feet down. All the houses on the hill are destroyed, and the world smells of natural gas. And there is a terrible sucking sound, like the earth is taking one long, deep wet breath.

I pedal as fast as I can down Lake Washington Boulevard which, strangely, is mostly intact. Fault lines. You never know what they'll tear up. Fallen trees litter the ground all around us. The world is devoid of electric lights, but full of light from fires that have ignited from gas lines and house fires. We snake our way through the carnage.

"Are you okay?" I call back to Joby, and I turn to look. He's in his bicycle stroller scared to death. "We'll be okay," I reassure him, though I'm not so sure myself.

Here's my logic: Beacon Hill, after a quake like that, is now Beacon Mound. Georgetown is the new waterfront. SoDo is a deep water bay. So no one is coming to help me and Joby. We have to help ourselves.

WE MAKE IT to Seward Park, which has become an island, an eventuality that I have anticipated. I blow up our little raft with the foot pump and paddle us over to Seward Island. We can see stuff, because the moon is out and the city is raging with fire. We get to the island and haul the raft up onto the shore. I tie the lengths of nylon rope to the safety rope that circles the raft. I don't know if it's going to work, but those parrots were trying to tell us something when they brought us the newspapers: an earthquake balloon boat. I grab a handful of peanuts and throw them high into the air.

"Polly want a peanut?" I yell.

And they appear. They hesitate, lurking in the trees, but I can see them. They don't take the peanuts; they're just as afraid as we are.

"We'll find some place," I tell them, "with trees and peanuts and dried mangos. We'll take you there."

I take the end of one of the ropes and put it in my mouth and then flap my arms. God, I hope this works. I'm pretty sure it will. After all, it was *their* idea. One of them lands near me and grabs a rope with his talons and lifts into the air. Okay, so talons are better than beaks. Whatever works. Thirty-nine other parrots join in. Joby and I climb into the boat, and they start flapping like mad. Suddenly we're flying.

PARROTS ARE exceptionally smart. They are also exceptionally strong fliers. They take turns on the ropes, doing a neat little rotation, so we always have about a hundred birds flying around us, forty of them doing the lifting. We fly through the night at about 300 feet, hovering over the carnage that was Seattle.

And it is carnage. Our bird raft circles north a bit, over the lake, and we see right away that both floating bridges are gone. We cross over the Mount Baker ridge and get a view of downtown, which is half the downtown it used to be, if that. Columbia Center is gone, as is the building that looks like a giant circumcised penis. Everything is glowing orange from fires, and the things that aren't glowing are black with flooded water: Puget Sound seems to have surged very high, maybe a tsunami. Harbor Island and all of SoDo are submerged and have become a new tidal flat. West Seattle is isolated, because the bridge has collapsed. I wonder where our dad is. I wonder about our mom. But there's no room in our bird raft for them anyway.

I point the birds south, and we follow I-5 as we fly along. Everything is dark. The entire coast, it seems. I have no idea how extensive the damage is or how far-ranging the quake. I turn the crank generator on my little survival radio and tune for a station, but I only get static. Finally, I get a weak signal.

"....devastation is absolute. There is nothing left. Nothing. The entire West Coast has fallen into the sea. We are the only station still broadcasting. If anyone can hear us, please come help. Please. We need help...."

We continue flying through the night with no known destination and just the kindness of a rag group of feral parrots to depend on. Joby looks up at me.

"When are we going to get there?" he asks.

I don't have the heart to tell him I'm not sure there's even a there to get to.

"Soon, Joby," I say. "We'll get there real soon."

Photo by Inti St. Clair.

Karen Finneyfrock's second book of poems, *Ceremony for the Choking Ghost*, was released from Write Bloody Publishing in 2010. Her young adult novel, *Celia, the Dark and Weird*, is due from Viking Children's Books, a division of Penguin Group, in Spring 2012.

Monster

KAREN FINNEYFROCK

Even the wet floor of the city bus, that slimy
torso, muddy with mountain spit, challenging each
rider's ankle to a duel, is romantic on an April afternoon.

I board in West Seattle, cross the bridge beneath
the eye of a volcano, pray an earthquake
doesn't come while we're on the viaduct,
sled the exit ramp into downtown, when
suddenly the bus driver stands on his brakes!

Rearing up on her hind legs in front of the bus,
two feet planted in the Puget Sound, yellow claws
tapping the tops of skyscrapers, stands Spring:

Godzilla with a head full of flowers, Gorgon with ivy
for snakes. She sniffs the bus, then sneezes, licks every tree twice.
She shoves her face in the ocean, shakes her dragon head in a pink fury;
rhododendrons rain over First Avenue.

The driver, terrified, turns up Pike, steps on the gas. We spill
our purses, fall into each other's laps. He knows Spring wants
to eat us like fat chickens, sucking the grease from our bones.
She wants to snap our spines before tossing us skulls first into
Summer. "Take them," she rages at her cousin-season, "they
always liked you better."

Monster of an adolescent girl,
Spring turns thirteen every year. She coats the city
in cherry blossoms so it will look like her messy bedroom,
laundry on the floor and phone ringing. She tosses punches filled
with pollen and wails, "I know that slut summer is coming
with her long legs and her easy love." Spring cries now and all the
hydrants on Pine Street explode, starts stomping up the staircase
of the city, "Mom, have you seen my sunglasses?" "Mom, I can't find my
    flip flops!"
She hates the color brown, hates boring things, loathes the way
    everyone
waits for summer with her brown skin and her pink blush. "I'm good
    enough,"
she sobs into the clouds. "If you loved me like you should love me,
I would stay here all year."

Spring's tears fall off and coat the bus like oil,
where they splash on the concrete moss and mushrooms
grow. She straightens up and steadies herself,
shakes out her hair and unclenches her hands. Tulips
fill the flowerbeds. When she leaves us, she goes
back to the ocean, through the Puget Sound.
Only the magnolia trees go with her.

Photo by Alicia Craven.

Laura Lichtenstein is nine years old going on ten and attends Broadview-Thompson Elementary School. One interesting thing about her family is that her mother is Chinese and her father is "slightly Yiddish." She likes fairies and spending time with her "true love," Levie. When it rains, Laura likes to read bedtime stories and play with her friends. Her biggest adventure was when she ran away to the White's house.

Starpoppy's Perfect Mate

LAURA LICHTENSTEIN

CHAPTER ONE: KING CROW'S PROCLAMATION

BLUEFEATHER JAY FLEW across Gold Desire Woodland and into Silver Grove Palace. Queen Grassweave and Maid Sparrow were hovering above King Crow. He was sick. They looked worried. Bluefeather Jay laid a purple flower on the King's lap as an antidote. Within the hour he felt much better.

"You have saved my life," King Crow said to Bluefeather Jay. "Prince Lovebird, my son, will marry your daughter, Starpoppy."

"I accept your offer," said Bluefeather Jay.

CHAPTER TWO: NO MORE FAMILY

STARPOPPY WOKE TO the sound of a gun. *Bang! Whack! Plop!*

"Quiet!" Starpoppy thought. Then a dead body plopped into the nest—it was her mother, Bluefeather Jay!

"Mama!" Starpoppy squawked. Just then, King Crow, sword in his talons, swooped over the nest, with Prince Lovebird right behind. King Crow grieved for his friend Bluefeather Jay. They had gone to school together.

Starpoppy was standing awkwardly in her ruffled white nightgown. She slowly advanced toward her mother's limp body and whispered, "I love you, Mom. Will I ever see you again? I have no family now."

HONK! *What was that!?* HONK! Starpoppy looked up, and a magnificent carriage was coming, followed by another. One of them had a yellow cross on the side. Inside the carriage, there was a goose wrapped in a shawl. The other carriage had two footmen, and jewels were engraved on its side. It had velvet seats. Starpoppy was escorted to the palace in tears.

CHAPTER THREE: THE PRINCE LOVES HER!

STARPOPPY FAINTED during the carriage ride. When she woke up, she was in the palace, and breakfast was laid on a side table—birdseed pancakes and nectar juice. Her sight was slightly foggy. She wasn't hungry, and her head hurt from fainting. She almost passed out again!

A few minutes later, she sat up, then stepped out of bed, feeling slippers on the floor. She put them on, and went over to the periwinkle closet. She opened it. *Oh my!* The most glittery and beautiful dresses in the world were sitting on hangers woven of leaves. Cautiously, she walked in and put one on. It was perfect. "I'm in heaven!" she thought, and put on a necklace. "What's that?" she wondered, gazing at a bottle of liquid. Maid Sparrow came in and sat cleaning the hearth. Starpoppy asked her what was in the bottle.

"Perfume, Dear," she replied. "It makes you smell good. This one makes you smell like clover nectar."

"Thanks," Starpoppy felt relieved.

"Any time," said Maid Sparrow, starting back to work. "And, Dear, Prince Lovebird is waiting for you in the room to your left." Prince Lovebird had fallen beak over talons in love with Starpoppy at the first sight of her, grieving for her mother in the nest.

Starpoppy left her bedroom and walked toward the room to her left. Along the marble hallway, excited whispers followed her: "Prince loves her!" "I wish I could inherit her luck!" "I wish I were Cupid, but then I couldn't marry him!" Starpoppy didn't know it, but she was wearing the romance dress!

"Your highness," she said with a curtsy when she saw him.

"No need for that, Princess Starpoppy Rhubarb Canary," replied Prince Lovebird.

"How do you know my full name?" asked Starpoppy.

"My father," he said.

"Oh," said Starpoppy.

"But why are we talking about this when we could be talking about...." he pulled aside the curtain.

A glittery tiara stood on a velvet pillow. The tiara was decorated with a crystal in the middle shaped like a snowflake. "Oh my, this is much too nice," Starpoppy thought.

Starpoppy realized that Prince Lovebird was lovebirding her! "Goodness! He loves me!" she thought.

CHAPTER FOUR: LET'S GET OUT OF HERE!

STARPOPPY, NOW DETERMINED to get Prince Lovebird a wedding gift, set off for the seashore! She didn't find a good shell, but what she did find was a castle made of sand—moat and all. The minute she climbed into the sand castle, she discovered she was trapped in a giant water bottle. All of a sudden, the water bottle was lifted away by its owner. Starpoppy was carried to a big house. In the distance, she could make out Gold Desire Woodland.

A few hours later...

Back at the castle, Prince Lovebird discovered that Starpoppy had been taken.

"Turtles, ready yourself for attack!" he cried. Prince Lovebird's order came out loud and clear. "Knights, onto your giant butterflies! Charge!" The turtles began shooting water pellets at everything that was made of bricks. The deer and the ponies trampled every creature in the way. The bucks and bulls rammed their horns into everything they could catch. The butterflies carried the knights to where Starpoppy was held. Starpoppy was rescued!

"Let's get out of here!" Prince Lovebird yelled.

"What a racket! Stop shooting everything!" Starpoppy gasped, then coughed out some dust.

Later...

"... Husband and wife!" finished Preacher Crane. Four leafed clovers came showering down! That night, Starpoppy took out her crown and gazed at it. Its snowflake crystal glistened in the moonlight.

David Shields is the author of twelve books, including *Reality Hunger: A Manifesto* (Knopf, 2010), which was named one of the best books of the year by more than thirty publications, and *The Thing About Life Is That One Day You'll Be Dead*, a *New York Times* bestseller. His work has been translated into fifteen languages.

Real Life

DAVID SHIELDS

THERE WAS A BLOG, then a Twitter feed, then a mega-selling book, and now a TV show (haven't seen it). It sounds too easy—someone just collecting the one-off wisdom of his father—but Justin Halpern's *Sh*t My Dad Says* is, to me, hugely about Vietnam (Samuel Halpern was a medic during the war), and on the basis of a single crucial scene, I think it's not inconsiderably about him still processing that violence, that anger. It's also hugely about being Jewish in America—again, very obliquely, mentioned just once; it's about the father teaching the son how to be Jewish and male in America, which is a contradictory, complicated thing.

Each entry is 140 characters or fewer—the length of a tweet. All of the subsections and mini-chapters are extremely short, and the book as a whole tries to have as thin a membrane as possible between writer and reader. It's essentially a tape recording of Sam's best lines, overdubbed with relatively brief monologues by Justin. It's not great or even good, probably, really, finally, but above all it's not boring. Which is everything to me. Compare it to, say, Franzen's *Freedom Fries*, whose high-church sonorities have zero to do with life now lived. (Franzen is, for me, the captain of the unfulfilled donnée. In *The Corrections*, he pretends to explore what is in fact a fascinating idea—that people, families, societies, and markets have a tendency to overcorrect—but he gives the merest lip service to unpacking this trope and settles instead for a painfully old-fashioned family album. *Freedom*: different metaphor; same result. Henry James said, "There is only one rule: never be boring." A huge number of novels are to me unconscionably boring. They don't have an idea in their head, and if they do, they do absolutely nothing with that idea.)

I don't want to read out of duty. There are hundreds of books in the history of the world that I love to death. I'm trying to stay alive and awake and not bored and not rote.

I'm not interested in preserving the repertory; I'm interested in a continuum of intellect. If you can't handle that distinction: Freud made up stories; go kill him.

What I love about *Sh*t My Dad Says* is the absence of space between the articulation and the embodiment of the articulation. The father, Samuel, is trying to teach his son that life is only blood and bones. The son is trying to express to his father his bottomless love and complex admiration. Nothing more; nothing less. There are vast reservoirs of feeling beneath Justin's voice and beneath his father's aphorisms.

The only mistake in the book is the final chapter, and it's a serious one. The mask comes off, and everything goes badly sentimental. It's a terrible move—almost certainly derived from editorial ham-fistedness. In many ways it ruins the book.

Sh*t My Dad Says could be a glimpse of a new form of book born out of the Facebook/MySpace/Twitter realm: Halpern's instinct was to make a blog first. The book seems to be a secondary recasting of the blog. It was the blog that people kept telling me about. I like that you can be an unemployed screenwriter in San Diego and six months later a best-selling writer.

Can social networking, blogging generate good books? In very rare occasions, such as this, yes. Justin Halpern says that he was collecting notes for a screenplay, then of course the notes became blog posts, the posts became tweets, the tweets became a website, book, TV show, etc.

Books, if they want to survive, need to figure out how to coexist with contemporary culture and catalyze the same energies for literary purposes. That cut-to-the-bone, cut-to-the-chase quality: this is how to write and read now.

The undergraduates I teach are much more open to a new reading experience when it's a blog. I know there have to be a hundred complex reasons as to why that is, but none of them change the fact that un- or even anti-literary types haven't stopped reading; they just don't get as excited about the book form. The blog form: immediacy, relative lack of scrim between writer and reader, promised delivery of unmediated reality, pseudo-artlessness, nakedness, comedy, real feeling hidden ten fathoms deep.

Another example: fifteen years ago, David Lipsky spent a couple of weeks with David Foster Wallace, then fourteen years later Lipsky went back and resurrected the notes. The resultant book, *Although Of Course You End Up Becoming Yourself*, pretends to be just a compilation of notes, and maybe that's all it is, but to me it's a meditation on two sensibilities: desperate art and pure commerce. Lipsky, I hope, knows what he's doing: evoking himself as the very quintessence of everything Wallace despised.

The book as such isn't obsolete; inherently, it's less immediate and raw, going as it does through the old-fashioned labyrinth of the publishing industry, and even when the book is printed and ready to go, you have to either get it at a store or have it shipped to you via Amazon. For now, this is a constraint we can work around. I take it as a challenge: to give a book a "live," up-to-date, awake, aware, instant feel. There will always be a place for, say, the traditional novel that people read on the beach or chapter by chapter at bedtime for a month as a means of entertainment and escape. There is, though, this other, new form of reading that most books being published today don't have an answer for. Even achieving a happy medium between the new and old reading experience is a great breakthrough.

Efficiency in the natural world: the brutal cunning of natural selection as it sculpts DNA within living organisms; DNA is always pushing towards the most efficient path to reproduction; water always finds the briefest, easiest path down hill. Concision is crucial to contemporary art: boiling down to the bare elements, reducing to just the basic notes (in both senses of the word). The paragraph-by-paragraph sizzle is everything.

A former student wrote me, "For years I've been taking notes and collecting quotes for a book that I hope will materialize at some point, but every time I attempt to turn the notes into the book, I hate the results. Really, what I've built is a database of little meditations, riffs, metaphors, and quotations. I find even my notes on how the book should be structured to be full of energy, because they're an outline of my massive aspirations, most of which I have no hope of actually pulling off. It feels almost as if my book wants to be about the planning of a book: a hypothetical literature that can't exist under earth's current gravity."

"The notes are the book," I wrote back, "I promise you."

Kaiz Esmail is nine years old and attends the University Child Development School. He is very intelligent and humorous. When it rains, he enjoys reading adventure books and user manuals, playing with his older (though not by much) twin sister and helping his parents. His biggest adventure took place when his family traveled to Belize and he rappelled down into a cave.

A Snowcapped Mountain...

KAIZ ESMAIL

WAY OFF, IN ANOTHER UNIVERSE, was Kai world. Kai world had snowcapped mountains, factories, parks, and much more. In this amazing world was the city of Esmont, the capital of Kai world. In Esmont, there was a bunch of mountains all clumped together. Near these mountains was a factory, which was called Snowy Mountain. Snowy Mountain manufactured ski lifts, skis, snowboards, gloves, ski suits, and anything else that had to do with skiing and snowboarding. Many people from all over the universe came to Esmont to ski and snowboard.

Also, in the same universe as Kai world, was Na world, Kai world's enemy. Na world wanted to invade Kai world. Na people wanted to melt all the snow and take over Kai world.

The kid president of Snowy Mountain was Nick. Nick was a blond-haired, blue-eyed boy who was twelve years old. He was a great skier and snowboarder.

"Nick! Can you bring me my hand warmers?" asked his mom.

"Sure, Mom."

"Thanks."

Every Sunday of every week, Nick and his family go skiing. All of them were great skiers. Nick started skiing when was three! Here is an entry from Nick's diary, which he wrote in the car going to ski:

Muharam 29, 1432

> *I am in the car going to ski. I am very bored. WAIT! I hear something on the radio! It says, "...snow is melting on the mountains! If all the snow melts, Kai world will flood! A big heater disguised as a plum from Na world is melting the snow! Somebody must stop the Na people! The plum looks like a regular plum, but it's huge."*

"Mom! Dad!" said Nick, "Hurry up! I've got to stop that heater!"

"Okay, okay, calm down. We're almost there," said his parents.

A few minutes later, Nick and his family reached the mountain. Nick took a ski lift up to the place where the heater was, but the Na people were guarding the heater. A wireless control panel was controlling the heater.

"Stop! Turn off that heater!" said Nick.

"NO! NO! NO!" said the Na people.

"Oh well," thought Nick, "I'll just have to find another way to stop that heater. If I could just see that control panel...."

"I have an idea! I'll use the spyware on my strapped-on computer to see the control panel!" Nick exclaimed to himself silently.

"ON. SELECT MODE. USE ˉ AND BUTTONS," read the screen. Nick selected spyware mode. He pointed the computer at the control panel and whispered, "Control panel." The screen read, "SEARCHING... SEARCHING...SEARCHING...," then it started beeping quietly and read, "FOUND! SHOWING PICTURE." Nick selected the zoom tool and zoomed in on the picture. In the right bottom corner of the control panel, it read, "WIRELESS CONNECTION STATUS: 100%, SECURITY: NOT PROTECTED."

"I have an idea! I will hack the wireless connection!" said Nick to himself.

Nick turned off the spyware mode and selected WIRELESS MODE. In the submenu, he selected HACK WIRELESS CONNECTION. Then he pressed SEARCH FOR CONNECTION. After the search, he selected HACK NA WIRELESS CONNECTION. The hack mode turned on, and a picture of the control panel for the plum heater showed up. Nick pressed SHUT DOWN FOREVER. A screen showed up, reading, "ARE YOU SURE? SELECT NO OR YES." Nick selected YES, then another screen showed up showing the progress: 0%...15%...30%...50%...70%...85%...87%... 90%...93%.. .95%...96%...98%...99%...100% COMPLETED!"

The heater shut down forever. Much to Nick's surprise, the Na people became frogs. Apparently the heater had been keeping the Na people in a human form. Nick became famous for saving Kai world, and the "frogs" lived happily on the mountain.

Photo by Chet Hay.

Kidus Solomon is seven years old and is a student at TOPS K-8 School. His family is Ethiopian and likes to play with each other. Kidus likes to read Calvin and Hobbes when it rains or go to Old Country Buffet to eat. His biggest adventure was when he was in Canada and saw a guy on a big unicycle balancing a baseball bat on his nose and juggling. One day Kidus would like to skydive from a plane and land in Old Country Buffet.

Monkeys Go Wild

KIDUS SOLOMON

"Ahhh! The gorillas escaped from the zoo!"
"Let's look for the gorillas!"
"You get a squad. Look in the gym."
"You get a squad. Look in the park."
"You get a squad. Look in my private yacht!"

The monkeys are on the Space Needle.
They are eating chocolate off a tree and clapping to lightning!

One monkey said, "I like chocolate off a tree!"

The second monkey said, "There is enough room for all the monkeys to go to the Space Needle!"

The third monkey said, "Let's go to the Space Needle!"

And the gorillas were at the Space Needle eating chocolate off a tree!

They finally found the gorillas in the Space Needle eating chocolate off a tree!

And the gorillas went back to the zoo!

Brenda Peterson is the author of sixteen books, including *Duck and Cover*, a New York Times Notable Book of the Year and the Northwest classic, *Living by Water: True Stories of Nature and Spirit*. This story is excerpted with permission from her new memoir, *I Want To Be Left Behind: Finding Rapture Here on Earth* (DaCapo Press, Boston, 2010). The Christian Science Monitor named the memoir among the "Top Ten Best Non-Fiction Books of 2010."

I Want to Be Left Behind

BRENDA PETERSON

"WITH 9/11, THE BLESSED COUNTDOWN for the Rapture has begun," my neighbor George informed me almost casually.

He caught me off guard. After decades of giddily anticipating the end of the world and getting no response from me, most of my relatives have stopped asking if I'm ready to be swept up midair with them. Plus, this was the last place I expected to be proselytized. George and I sat perched on driftwood, keeping watch over a seal pup that had hauled up onto our backyard Salish Sea shore, just south of Alki Beach. Our Seattle community beach is precious to harbor seals—a place where they can give birth, nurse, rest. Late summer through September, mother seals leave their pups here while they fish. We neighbors stay the respectful one hundred yards away from the pup, as advised by the Marine Mammal Protection Act, keeping watch on the vulnerable pups in shifts of usually four hours. It's a startling stretch of time to spend together with people we usually whiz past in our busy lives.

"Hmmmmm," I answered in a whisper, hoping that my neighbor would lapse into the companionable silence we usually enjoy together while seal sitting, as we call our beach communion. "Hand me the binoculars, will you?"

This pup was about two feet long, round and robust, its speckled fur camouflaged against the rocky beach. He was breathing regularly, with no yellow discharge from mouth or nose—all good signs. We didn't see any wounds, such as orca bites, propeller gashes, or bullet holes. But he could have suffered some internal injuries. Only careful observation and time would reveal his fate. If the pup is injured or doesn't leave the beach after forty-eight hours, we call our marine mammal stranding expert, Kristin Wilkinson, at NOAA (National Oceanic and Atmospheric Administration), who may authorize someone to remove the seal to a rehab shelter for treatment. Though Washington State has a thriving seal population, 50 percent of juveniles do not survive their first year, and every seal season we neighbors witness seal pup deaths.

George and I were sitting second shift, studying the pup's body language: can he lift flippers and head in the agile "banana position" to scan for predators and mother? Our most important job as seal-sitters is to shoo dogs and overly curious people politely away from the pup, partly because diseases are communicable among the three species. We also chat with other neighbors and passersby and educate them in seal etiquette. If the mother returns and finds her pup surrounded by too much human activity, she may abandon her baby.

"This pup looks plump and healthy, don't you think?" I asked George in a whisper.

"I sure hope so," he murmured.

Violet mists floated just above the waves like ghost ships. Suddenly, a foghorn moaned in baritone blasts, and the seal pup shuddered. He lifted his head, his black eyes huge, his tiny ear slits opened wide, listening.

"That's how it'll happen, you know," George said quietly. There was a note of triumph in his tone. "The trumpets will sound, and we'll be lifted up far away from here."

For a moment I considered not engaging in this loopy, no-exit dialogue.

But because this was my neighbor, not my family, I simply smiled. George and I had a lot of time and a seal pup on our hands. No way out. "Listen, George," I began. "Why are you so ...well ...cheerful about the end of the Earth?"

This gave him a moment's pause. Then he said, with some chagrin, "You can't blame us born-agains for wanting at last to get our heavenly rewards. We've waited thousands of years."

His dark eyes flashed a familiar fire I'd seen in preachers' faces during my Southern Baptist childhood. As I watched the seal pup settle back into his vigilant scanning of the waves, his belly rising and falling in those deep drafts of breath that only the very young of any species seem to enjoy, I persisted. "Why would you want this world to end, George? What's the hurry?"

I could see that my neighbor was now studying me as if I were the seal pup, as if he had already passed me in the slow sinner's lane on the freeway to the Apocalypse. "The hurry is that right now we see signs and wonders proving that the End Times are upon us," George insisted. "We've got holy wars, world financial markets crashing, Israel's military power, Islamic terrorists, and even global warming." This last sign he pronounced brightly, as if our global climate was gleefully graduating into a hot time in the old world.

I wanted out of the conversation. I felt claustrophobic in the tight grip of my neighbor's End Times intensity. Oddly, I wondered if my restlessness was like the anxiety fundamentalists seem to feel about the whole world, as if they are trapped by the original gravity of their sins. Or perhaps to the Rapture hopefuls, the Earth's fall into global warming signals that our world has become what they always suspected—hell, the "fire next time." Perhaps their Rapture prophecy is a kind of biblical lullaby to calm their environmental terrors. As one relative member assured me, "There are no drowning polar bears and melting ice caps where I'm going."

It struck me that being "raptured" out of this world trumps the insecurity of living and the surrender of dying. No bodily indignity. No suffering.

One will simply be whisked off with the fellowship of the believers, the Rapture gang, to a heavenly and just reward. In the twinkling of an eye, they say, the righteous will ascend, dropping golden dental work, night-gowns, and perhaps some spouses. Unless you count losing the Earth and billions of unfortunate sinners who cling to it, getting raptured is a blast. Who wouldn't want to escape the prophesied plagues of locusts, frogs, and killer viruses, an Earth overwhelmed by tsunamis, volcanoes, and nomadic legions of the unsaved?

"Sandwich, George?" I rummaged in my backpack for a pimento cheese sandwich. Though I've backslid from my mother's Southern Baptist religion, I still carry on her fabulous food rituals.

My neighbor shook his head. His hunger was spiritual. Not to be put off, he told me, "I'm afraid you'll have a rough time of it here during the Tribulations."

"Don't you love any of us who will suffer in those Tribulations?" I asked. "Those of us you leave behind?"

George took my arm a little too tightly. "But you could come with us to meet Jesus midair in the Rapture. You could escape all the Tribulations—and wait for the Second Coming to return here. Then Christ will defeat the Anti-Christ and establish His kingdom. Then the Earth will be pure again."

George was closing in, just as surely as the tide was rising, surf coming closer to the seal pup's small, whiskered snout. I politely disengaged. It was enough that I had to contend with some friends who calculate that by the end of the Mayan calendar in 2012 all civilizations will either be spiritually transformed or destroyed. And of course, some of my most extreme green comrades are convinced the Earth will be a more pristine place without people. Given this Greek chorus of apocalypse, what was one more vision of the Last Days?

I hid behind my huge binoculars. But I really was a little worried. It had been twelve hours since the discovery of this pup. In a few more hours it would be high tide again. Where was the mother?

George rummaged in his backpack and pulled out his laptop. He often brings his home office to the beach while seal sitting. We can tap into dozens of wireless haloes shimmering unseen around nearby apartments. "I'm sending you this link," George said. "It's the home page for the non-raptured."

Squinting in the morning marine light, I could barely make out the computer screen, which read: "Inheriting from the Raptured." A very official last will and testament followed: "Contact your saintly friends now. Offer to let them use the convenient form below to keep their fiscal assets from slipping into the hands of Satan's One World Government agents."

"But, George," I protested. "This site isn't serious."

"It doesn't matter if it's joking," George insisted. "It will still work."

I saw that the will had blank signature lines marked "Infidel Witness #1" and "Infidel Witness #2." "Well, I suppose," I suggested with a smile, "that we can ask some of the other seal-sitters to witness this for us."

"Yeah, we can do this together."

Then I remembered I had seen his car boasting a new bumper sticker: In case of Rapture, this car will be unmanned. I had wanted to tell him that I was going to get a new bumper sticker too: In case of Rapture, can I have your car?

Now here he was, my dear neighbor, actually signing me up to inherit his worldly possessions—his world.

I was strangely touched.

With a pang I realized that while some End-Timers may not have the stamina and constancy for compassion, for "suffering with," many, like George and my family, feel real concern for the infidel loved ones they will abandon. And watching George's expectant face, I reminded myself that his spiritual stewardship, like that of some other evangelicals, did include other species and the natural world. Not long before, George had built a floating platform for an injured pup so she could find sanctuary offshore while salt-water and sun healed a gash she received from a boat propeller. Anchored by another neighbor's boat buoy, this "life raft" became a refuge for many other resting and nursing seals. One of the seal-sitters, Susan, actually witnessed a pup's birth on that raft. An eagle swooped down, taking up the placenta and afterbirth in her talons. But the newborn and mother seal floated safely below.

George has also helped me bury the pups who don't survive each season. We are trained to bury them deep under beach sand so their bodies can nourish the whole ecosystem. Once we seal-sitters had the sorrowful task of burying a pup as the mother swam back and forth in the surf, calling and cooing to her newborn to come back to her. The mother's moans stay in my mind these many months later.

"Oh, look," George exclaimed in a whisper and snapped shut his laptop. "He's up!"

Our pup intently scanned the waves for his mother and the beach for predators. For the first time, he fixed his full attention on us. Through the detached intimacy of binoculars, I could see that his breathing had steadied and he was actually rolling over on his side into a more relaxed and natural position. As he lifted his front flipper up to scratch his whiskers, his huge eyes held mine with that unblinking gaze that is at once wild and very familiar. After all, seals are our mammal kin. In coastal cultures all over the world, they are said to be shape-shifters, selkies, shedding their seal skins onshore to become human, if only for a night, a nuptial, a haunting reverie.

George and I tracked the seal pup's every move—and now there were many. Repeatedly, he lifted his head and hind flippers to scan the waves and beach, then scratched, scooted, rolled over, and gave a long, leisurely yawn.

If, over the hours spent hauled out, seals are protected, we've actually seen their initial wariness relax into deep naps. The seals know we are near, and because we do not approach they find some peace. And so do we. How often are we humans privileged to watch an animal dream beside us?

Even when a seagull nipped at his tail flukes, the pup barely stirred. Fast asleep, he was dreaming through the late-afternoon dissonance of commuter traffic, rap music, some schoolboys' Frisbee contest. Was the pup certain his mother would return? Was George this sure of the Rapture?

"George," I suggested, "why don't you take a break? Go join your family for supper."

"Anytime now," George murmured, "the mother will return. That's my favorite part."

And then I understood something about my neighbor and about myself. All of us know what it feels like to wait for someone to call, finally to come home, to recognize our love, to reunite with those of us who long for something more, something greater than ourselves. Maybe it will come in the night, in that twinkling of an eye. Maybe it will save us from a lonely beach.

As if in answer to our longing, a glossy head popped up far out in the waves. The seal pirouetted to find her pup on the beach. George and I sat absolutely still, hardly breathing. A soft cooing call from the mother. The pup fairly leapt up, flippers unfurling like wings. Flop, flop, flop, and then an undulant body-hop along beach stones as the pup inched toward the surf.

"Ah, you're safe now, buddy," George sighed, as the seal pup slipped into the waves and swam as fast as his tiny flippers could carry him back to his mother. There was tranquillity in George's face, a sweet calm that often comes from sitting on the beach all day with nothing to do but watch over a fellow creature. From our driftwood seat, we saw the two seals dive and disappear. Nearby, comic black-and-white harlequin ducks popped up in the waves. Even though our seal sitting was over, we didn't move. A great blue heron swooped in with the caw of a dinosaur bird. How could this ancient bird fly with such huge wings? How did she escape extinction? Somehow the great blue had adapted beautifully.

The driftwood creaked slightly under our weight. It was a madrona log, its soft ruby bark peeling from years lost at sea. I surprised myself by going back to the subject I had worked so hard to avoid. I asked George, "What if we're sitting here to make sure that there will be something left for our kids?"

He seemed to ponder this for a while. "You're a really good neighbor, George," I told him. "We would all miss you so much if you zipped up to heaven. We'd all say, 'Well, there goes the neighborhood!'"

George took the compliment in stride. Along with seal sitting, he also participates in our neighborhood block watch. He is someone I might call upon in an emergency, unless, of course, that emergency was the Rapture.

"I'll miss you," George admitted, "and... and all this too."

"You know, George," I said softly, "I really want to be left behind."

My neighbor looked at me thoughtfully and then fell quiet as we watched another harlequin float past, bright beak dripping a tiny fish. Happy, so happy in this moment. The great blue cawed hoarsely and stood on one leg in a fishing meditation. Wave after bright wave lapped the beach, and the summer sunset glowed on our faces. We sat in silence, listening to waves more ancient than our young, hasty species, more forgiving than our religions, more enduring. Rapture.

Excerpted from I Want to Be Left Behind: Finding Rapture Here on Earth (*DaCapo Press, Boston, 2010*).

Rebeka Berhanu is nine years old and attends Daniel Bagley Elementary School. She is an excellent cookie baker, and excels at math and drawing. When it rains, she likes to read the *Diary of a Wimpy Kid* series, jump in rain puddles, or stay home and eat popcorn. Her biggest adventure was when she visited San Francisco.

The Whale in the Swimming Pool

REBEKA BERHANU

ONCE UPON A TIME there was a girl named Emily, and she went to a swimming pool to swim. When she went in, a whale appeared! It was a big whale, and it was as big as a spaceship. Emily couldn't believe her eyes. Emily jumped out of the pool as quickly as she could. The whale said, "Why are you running away from me?"

"Oh my God!" Emily said. "You can talk."

"Yeah," the whale said.

"But animals can't talk. It's impossible," Emily said.

Then Emily went away and felt really weird. She went home, and the whale came again and said, "Can you take me to the Pacific Ocean to get back home?"

"Okay," said Emily.

Then they left to go to the Pacific Ocean. While they were getting there, the whale didn't know how to walk, so Emily had to roll him down the road. Emily suddenly tripped and the whale rolled away. Emily ran as fast as she could to catch the whale. She jumped on the whale and started to ride on it. After a while, they made it to an ocean, but they didn't know what kind of ocean. They thought that they were at the Pacific Ocean.

But they weren't at the Pacific Ocean. They were at the Atlantic Ocean, so they had to walk the other way to find the Pacific Ocean. Thirty hours later they found another ocean and they found out that this time, they were at the Pacific Ocean. So Emily dropped off the whale and went back to the swimming pool to swim. When Emily was done swimming, she missed the whale. But she couldn't go to the Pacific Ocean because she was tired and she knew that it would take more than thirty hours to get there. So she went home.

Photo by Chet Hay.

Zoë Newton is eleven years old and attends St. John School. She enjoys going on boat rides with her siblings. When it is raining, Zoë enjoys reading absolutely anything, and talking with her family, and spending time with her 17 pets, and going to Pike Place Market. Her biggest adventure was when she hiked around the Olympic Peninsula. One day, Zoë would love to hike to Reflection Lake on Mount Rainier, listening to drops of rain on the water while taking a hungry bite into a big cinnamon roll.

The Peacock Suit

ZOË NEWTON

I LIVED IN the McGuire apartment building downtown on the twenty-first floor when my family and I were informed that the demolition company was going to implode the building because it was structurally unsound. I remember that day clearly. They told us we had to move, as the rain pounded and lashed the windows. We only had a few weeks to decide where to go. After a while we found a yellow house with peeling paint that seemed depressing and desolate, even after we moved in all our furniture. The house also reminded me how much I would miss the Experience Music Project, a music museum also known as the EMP.

The EMP was only a ten minute walk from the McGuire, so I took a stroll there often. Some time in January I spent every cent of my allowance on a one-year membership. I didn't want the membership to go to waste after I moved, so I began taking the bus there during the summer.

One day I was walking to the bus stop when a tall girl with frizzy red hair crashed her bike into me. I fell backward onto the ground, as the girl hopped off her bike to help me. "Are you alright?" she asked, holding out her hand to help me. "I'm Trigoni."

"I'm Adrian," I replied. "Well, this is something I would not expect on a casual walk to the bus stop."

"Oh, you're taking the bus?" Trigoni said curiously. "Where to?"

"My favorite place in the universe," I answered, "the EMP. I used to go all the time until we had to move to Greenwood." (I admit I added the last part out of a desire for sympathy.)

"The EMP?" Trigoni's face lit up. "Can I go with you? I once went with my brother, and we stayed so late we were locked in. Then, we heard Jimi Hendrix arguing with Elvis Presley. Hendrix wanted to try on Elvis's peacock jumpsuit, but Elvis said, You can't, we're dead!'"

I nodded slowly, wanting to believe this girl wasn't crazy. Something told me that if she was right, it might take my mind off living so far away from my favorite place ever. "Okay," I said finally. "Let's go."

We walked Trigoni's bike home and continued toward the bus stop. On the way, she ran her mouth a mile a minute—about every exhibit at the EMP, like the tower made of guitars, the music room, and the Jimi Hendrix exhibit. She continued while we waited for the bus, then came to an abrupt stop when it arrived. I showed the driver my bus pass, and Trigoni gave him seventy-five cents.

As the bus headed south, I gazed at the sun shimmering on Green Lake and thought about Trigoni's story. Was the EMP really haunted? Why would Jimi Hendrix want to try on Elvis's jumpsuit? What *was* the peacock suit?

After the bus came to our stop, we had to walk a bit. When we got to the EMP, Trigoni paid for a ticket and I used my membership card. Just like all the other times I've been here, the whole place took my breath away. The sound of acoustic guitars danced in my ears, while I looked at every instrument in sight. I didn't bother reading the descriptions because I knew most of them by heart.

When we reached the live music performance, I listened intently, concentrating on every note pounding in my ears.

It was about four o' clock when we decided to leave. As Trigoni and I headed for the exit, we passed a picture of Jimi Hendrix. I stopped to look at it. Suddenly, his face became...animated. He winked at me and raised his hand. He rotated his finger clockwise, and I felt wind blowing around me, and everything—even my mind—began to move very fast.

Then the wind stopped and the room went dark. I could faintly see the outline of Trigoni's shocked expression. I stared at the photo of Jimi Hendrix—only Jimi Hendrix wasn't there. I whipped my head around in every direction, and then heard a deep voice in my ear.

"In case you're wondering, us older ghosts have the power to make time go by quicker than usual." I turned around, and Trigoni and I shrieked in unison. Jimi Hendrix was standing behind us, grinning as if he were very pleased with himself. He was wearing a tunic and bell bottom pants. Every part of him was pearly white, from his hair to his skin to his clothes, which added extra creepiness.

"You seem like a smart girl." Jimi remarked to me. "Do you think I would look good in the Elvis Presley peacock suit?"

"I...uh..." I stuttered in shock.

"Oh give it a rest, Hendrix!" said another voice. "I know your plan!" A man with black cowlicked hair floated toward Trigoni and me. He was wearing a white jumpsuit with a peacock painted on it, its tail wrapping majestically around the leg. The King of Rock 'n' Roll.

"I know you only want to steal my favorite suit!" Elvis bellowed. "Don't think you're being a sly dog! 'Cause you ain't nothin' but a hound dog!"

Trigoni laughed.

"Well, Elvis. I could just be wanting to try it on," Jimi said defensively.

"Okay! Stop arguing!" I shouted angrily. "Elvis, how about you let him try it on. Then he can take it off and give it back. Does that seem fair?"

They both muttered something that sounded like, "Oh sure, I guess."

Elvis disappeared and reappeared holding the peacock suit and wearing jeans and a leather jacket.

Jimi rushed over and put on the peacock suit. He danced around a bit, and Elvis sighed impatiently. "Okay, can you give it back now?"

Jimi smiled deviously and suddenly dashed out the door.

Elvis looked at me furiously and said, "Great idea!" He grabbed Trigoni and me by and collars and threw us out the door.

Then everything went black.

I WOKE UP to the sound of dramatic beeping. I was in the hospital.

"Adrian!" Trigoni said when she saw I was awake. "We were at the EMP, and you were looking at this picture of Jimi Hendrix, then you passed out!"

"Trigoni, there's something else you should hear." I told her about my dream.

"Do you know what this means?" Trigoni asked abruptly. "Jimi Hendrix and The King communicated with you through your dream!" She looked at me triumphantly.

I stared at her.

"Trigoni," I said finally. "You're crazy."

Photo by Alicia Craven.

Kaley Walgren is nine years old. She plays the violin and her family has a cabin in the Hood Canal. When it rains, she likes to read poetry and splash in puddles at Golden Gardens Park. If she could go on any adventure, it would be to a rain forest to see owls, armadillos, tree frogs, and geckos.

Drowning in a Current

KALEY WALGREN

You feel
You're floating,
Swirling,
Around and around.
You don't feel rushed, and your mind's relaxed.
You sink slowly down.
You don't swim up or down.
Neither.
You just look up at the light right above you.
You sit there and you listen
For the muffles of voices above you.
And vanish.

Samuel Wade is ten years old and goes to Broadview-Thomson. He likes sports and playing video games. When it rains, he likes to read sad books. His biggest adventure was when he went to Disneyland.

The Robot Chicken

SAMUEL WADE

ONCE THERE WAS a chicken who was mentally ill (crazy in the mind). The farmer had to take it to the hospital. The doctors took out the infected half of his brain and replaced it with a robotic half.

When the chicken came out of the hospital, he was half chicken, half robot. When he got back to his barn, the chicken stepped into the barn and all of the animals ran away from him.

The robot chicken went back to his coop and sat in the corner. The other chickens in the coop were making fun of him. He got mad and all of the sudden a laser shot from his eyes. *PWWWWWWWW!* Smoke was everywhere. When the smoke went away, there was nothing left in the coop. The robot chicken had accidentally disintegrated the rest of the flock.

"Where did everyone go?" he asked, confused. "I guess I zapped them with my laser eyes!"

Just then, Farmer Fred walked in and looked at the coop. Farmer Fred was famished and looking forward to his chicken dinner. "Looks like I'm gonna have to cut off your head," said Farmer Fred, picking up the robot chicken by his legs and taking him to a tree stump.

Farmer Fred was about to chop through the robot chicken's neck, but then *PWWWWWWWW!* The ax head went flying.

"What the?" said Farmer Fred, in shock.

Where did the ax head go? thought the robot chicken.

The farmer took the robot chicken back to his coop.

"I'll be back with a new ax," said Farmer Fred, closing the barn door. When Farmer Fred was gone, all the other animals in the barn asked the robot chicken what had happened. The robot chicken was confused, and still a bit in shock. He said nothing and just sat there.

An hour later, Farmer Fred returned. The robot chicken was cleaning himself in his coop and didn't notice Farmer Fred coming into the barn.

"I'm baaack," said the farmer. The farmer startled the robot chicken, who turned suddenly to face him. *PWWWWWWWWWW!* Lasers again shot from the robot chicken's eyes. Farmer Fred vanished in an instant, leaving behind a tuft of smoke and the smell of fried chicken. The robot chicken was disgusted.

Where did he go? thought the robot chicken. He was confused for a moment, but then he had an idea. "Oh well. Now we can at least have some fun," he said. With that, a disco ball dropped from the barn roof and music started to play. All of the horses, cows, donkeys, and the dog started to dance.

"This song has a great beat!" said the robot chicken.

"That's not the beat!" said the horse. "That's someone knocking at the barn door. Get this stuff down before we're caught, everyone!" After hearing the horse's warning, the animals scattered to turn off the music and take down the disco ball. They all ran back to their pens just as the barn door opened. It was the farmer's daughter, Lisa.

"Where did daddy go?" Lisa said sobbing. "He said he would go fishing with me," she said, wiping her nose. The animals felt sorry for poor Lisa, so they jumped over their gates and snuggled her, except for the robot chicken because he was afraid he would accidentally zap her legs.

The next morning, the robot chicken had another surprise—he'd grown to be bigger than the barn! "Woops! I crushed the barn," he said. He ran into the city. When he walked, cars crashed. The ground rumbled when he ran.

He went to City Hall and asked if he could help the city. Mayor Bob said yes. The robot chicken spent the rest of his life helping people and became a hero. Two years later, he died and the townspeople made a statue of him. The townspeople visited the statue every day to place flowers by his feet. Today, they continue to believe that the robot chicken's spirit lives on inside the statue.

Northwest Field Recording A/B Mix, Victoria Haven, 2010
Courtesy of Victoria Haven and PDX Contemporary Art, Portland. © Victoria Haven

3

CONNECTIONS

Photo by Mary Randlett.

Frances McCue likes to read Baudelaire in the mists of Seattle. Her books include two volumes of poetry, *The Stenographer's Breakfast* and *The Bled,* and a book of essays about Richard Hugo and Northwest towns, *The Car That Brought You Here Still Runs.*

Poems

FRANCES McCUE

— *Adult Life* —

I wanted to brush his hair. I did not love him. I had come on business, and we spent time in meetings, waiting our turns at coffee urns, in and out of hotel conference rooms.

I wanted to brush his hair. It was a smooth gloss, folded into his ponytail. I had come on business and we spent time together as one does on business. His hair looked dusted in the dull light.

I wanted to brush his hair. This would not help him. He took care of his hair on his own. I know, as I do when I'm on business, that all men do not need women to help them.

I wanted to brush his hair. I had come on business, and I was not to care for him. I waited, as one does on business, until the time passed and he had found his own way while I fell asleep with the hotel TV on, dreaming of his hair.

I wanted to brush his hair. It was his hair, and I wanted to take some part in it. This did not mean I loved him. I had come on business, and I cared for him the way one cares for another child.

I wanted to brush his hair. We were together. I did not love him. Like a child I wanted to braid it and say, "Sit still," until someone came to fetch us.

The business I came for left me wanting to brush his hair. In the beginning of the business, his hair meant nothing. It distracted me, until brushing it seemed like my work, the work I came to do.

I wanted to brush his hair, you see, all of it. Through the bristles, I'd pull the hair like a luscious weaving, all texture and intent. The hair would pass through like streams of people through turnstiles, all the people he might be. I would not love him as I conducted this.

I wanted to brush his hair. I did not love the hair, or him. But I wanted to lay my hands there, and know it could be without affection. That hair meant nothing to me. I wanted to brush it. I had hands, and a brush nestled in my purse. He was right there in front of me and I was all business.

— *Seattle Architect* —

Foghorns, railway whines, tin lifts for grain and gravel,
old machinery—
a rainstorm drive through the industrial heart.
I'm aiming for the site.
In this city's maritime end, where container loads
wait for Monday's
shipping lines, I'm wondering: "Will my sketches match the place?"
Months, I've been
drawing this building. I re-sketched every arc, turned
transepts into beams,
carved doorways from the walls. The blueprints, clean and smooth,
roll along the seat.
Will the structure fit the un-squared lot, the dark-vine hill?
I draw the place
from oddities, bumps in the earth,
and start anew
each time I come here. Forever, I could spin between
paper and the place.
The prints, teased with angles and arcs sharp and smooth—
ivory laced with blue—
never match this site. I've been here more than I'd like.
I steer the truck,
clattering over gravel, underneath the half-framed bulk.
From arc to arch,
there's a heady spin: you travel from *whim* to *made thing*.

Photo by Raymond Gendreau.

S.J. Weinberg lives on Bainbridge Island, Washington, and teaches writing classes at the Art Institute of Seattle. His writing:includes short stories, personal essays, travel essays, and a novel under construction. Some of his tales have been published in small magazines, and several fictions are featured on a down-home podcast produced at wordjam.podomatic.com. ·

Kissing the Tarantula

S. J. WEINBERG

I WAS KISSING MY TARANTULA Rodriguez, named for a boyhood friend who succumbed to the influenza fifteen years ago when we were nine years old. Since then, I've graduated from college and have been working behind the counter at Federico's Medical Supply Shop, where my specialty is bandages. I know about all kinds of bandages, whether for wounds or for support of strained muscles. Such is the fate of having a degree in twentieth century Dutch literature, with a focus upon the novels of Cees Nooteboom. Prospective employers laugh at me in interviews. People here crack up at the mere mention of Dutch literature. Only Tonya, Federico's old sister, who looks to be in her late seventies, though she may be younger—with her severely bony face, pointy nose, deep-set eyes, and bushy eyebrows, and coffee-stained teeth that make her appear ancient and bloodless—has ever understood my passion for Dutch stories, poems, folk literature, and contemporary novels; and she was the one who put her foot down, insisting that Federico hire me. So, with a cockeyed smirk and a what-the-hell tip of his head, he conceded and gave me a position behind the bandage counter.

I was kissing my tarantula Rodriguez, named for a boyhood friend who succumbed to the influenza fifteen years ago when we were nine years old.

Since graduating from college, I have been working behind the counter at Federico's Medical Supply Shop, where my specialty is bandages. I know about all kinds of bandages, whether for wounds or for support of strained muscles. Such is the fate of having a degree in twentieth century Dutch literature, with a focus upon the novels of Cees Nooteboom. Prospective employers laugh at me in interviews. People here crack up at the mere mention of Dutch literature. Only Tonya, Federico's old sister, who looks to be in her late seventies, though she may be younger—with her severely bony face, pointy nose, deep-set eyes and bushy eyebrows, and coffee-stained teeth that make her appear ancient and bloodless—has ever understood my passion for Dutch stories, poems, folk literature, and contemporary novels; and she was the one who put her foot down, insisting that Federico hire me. So, with a cockeyed smirk and a what-the-hell tip of his head, he conceded and gave me a position behind the bandage counter.

I was kissing my tarantula Rodriguez, my little pal I bring to work in a bamboo cage, when Tonya approached with a demitasse cup of coffee in one bony little hand and a cigarette dangling from the corner of her thin, dry lips. "He's a cute one, no? There's something deep and intelligent about your furry friend." I put Rodriguez back in his cage and latched the top. If it had been anyone else, I'd have assumed the comment's intent would be to raise my ire, but Tonya was constitutionally sincere, incapable of gratuitous meanness.

"Yes, somewhere in there is a little boy who was my friend long ago, more like a brother, really, a confidant and fellow dreamer. Then the influenza traveled down from the stars and infected him with a fever that cooked his brain and invaded his heart and deposited him in the dark earth before he ever had a chance to live."

She nodded and took a long cheek-sucking draw on her cigarette, releasing a billowing puff of grey smoke into the air above her. "May I kiss him?" I'd never had anyone ask to kiss my tarantula, and I didn't know how

I felt about it. I liked Tonya, regarded her like a special old aunt, thought of her as much more than my employer; she was a kindred spirit. But Rodriguez knew my secrets, knew my fears, knew my aspirations. I didn't want to say no, but I wasn't sure I was ready to say yes. Even to Tonya.

We stood silently together behind the counter, listening to the sounds of Rodriguez slowly scaling the sides of his cage. I knew this wasn't my boyhood friend Rodriguez; he was long dead, and I was no longer the boy who had known him, but on another level I always felt that the tarantula actually was that missing brother.

II

WHEN WE WERE BOYS, just after my father became deathly ill and tired as his heart grew large and his lungs began filling with water, I had no one. My mother tried, but her overwhelming grief weighed upon her, often driving her to her bed for days at a time. She could hardly keep herself going. My new friend Rodriguez filled a gap; he replaced my missing father and my distant mother. He couldn't have been more perfect if I'd invented him myself. He was real though, and his mother seeing how vulnerable and angry and frightened I had become about my crumbling world, treated me like a second son—like an adopted son; with a motherly kind of love, Lilianna became a protector and someone who genuinely cared for me. She would rest her hand on my head and smile at me and invite me to eat with Rodriguez when she would make him lunch, or would offer me lime soda and bananas when Rodriguez and I would come running in from playing soccer or from riding our bikes through the warren of dirt roads in the forest of mangled trees beyond the Café Con Leche River.

When my father became bedridden and my mother nearly sank into catatonia, Lilianna often put an arm around me and would press me to her bosom. Rodriguez's mother made me feel I had a home when my family began falling irreparably apart. And eventually, even to my actual mother's relief, I moved in and shared Rodriguez's small bedroom, sleeping on a cot Lilianna padded with old quilts and made comfortable for me with animal pillows—giraffes and bears and crocodiles to support my sad, confused head. I had no idea at the time that not only would she become a surrogate for my vanishing family, but I would become a surrogate for her Rodriguez.

III

COLD WHITE STARS sharply delineated peculiar constellations in the blackest winter sky that season that snatched Rodriguez from Earth, from Lilianna's heart, and from a large portion of my darkening soul. That was the year I learned that when people say it can't get any worse, that certainly it can always get worse—worse than anyone might ever imagine, worse than anyone dare contemplate. Friendship, family, love, and loss all serve to define permanence and impermanence; and mortality and the objective world made of skin and flesh and bone and the materials that can be seen, heard, tasted, touched, smelled, and otherwise perceived sometimes consort to torture a boy as they did when I was nine and alone in infinity— except for Lilianna, who now understood me and knew the depths of my sorrow, because her loss and mine were limitless and awful, but sometimes tolerable only because we had each other.

IV

I KNOW THAT most people fear the night, but Lilianna and I felt relief when the activity of day swooned away into darkness. The illuminations of life were too painful, reminded us of too much; and night dampened the pain, quieted the mind and narrowed our sorrows to the objects of their wrenching ardor in ways that our companionship could almost tolerate, even if we couldn't rationally comprehend them. Many people find distraction from mourning and loss in the brightness of daily activity. For us, daylight meant the excruciating possibility of painful shadows at every turn.

We became inhabitants of night for seven years. It took that long to come out from under the covers, for our wounds to heal enough to face dawn and the freshness of new days. I was sixteen when we emerged, but with the deep-set eyes and dour mouth of a man.

We had lived in books, had sat quietly listening to the radio, had cooked simple meals we ate slowly, observing steam rising from our plates and bowls. Lilianna taught me to drink wine, instructed me in the skills of cleaning, cooking, and, most importantly, of listening and conversing. We talked, but mostly we listened as we waited. And then the day arrived when she came into my room, once Rodriguez's bedroom, and she shook my shoulder, told me to dress, that we were going out to shop for vegetables in the town market.

The heat and light and traffic and human hustle and bustle felt like an assault at first. I wanted to cover my ears and close my eyes. But I gradually heard the music and rhythms that make humans step with purpose and curiosity to the beat of the heart. Life returned. Lilianna's face relaxed. I went back to school and even participated in the lives of other teenagers. In the evenings, like an old couple, Lilianna and I would talk about the activities of our day. I never mentioned my father or mother. I wasn't capable of that. And we never spoke of Rodriguez. We just couldn't.

V

ON NOVEMBER FIRST, my eighteenth birthday, things changed. Lilianna was up to something unusual. There was a way she was silent that became a dead giveaway. We had spent so many dark, silent seasons together that I knew she was planning something. When she wished to conceal her mind, the ways she monitored her movement, suppressed her facial expressions, paused to examine me, always spilled the beans that she was designing a secret event for me. In the past, it might have been an extraordinary chocolate cake or a present of a book she knew I wanted. I was older now, and she moved in ways that indicated she was up to something serious, something originating deep in her heart.

I'd been accepted to go to the university, so I thought her secrecy might have something to do with honoring that. And I was pretty sure she would make an especially delicious wild-mushroom lasagna for me; I'd been dropping hints about lasagna for weeks.

That night, I returned home at the usual dinner time, eight p.m., and when I opened the door, I saw our apartment decorated in flowers and lit with candles. The table was set with a floral tablecloth, our best plates and silverware and glassware, and twenty small porcelain bowls of appetizers and condiments. And sitting at the table, in a black dress buttoned up to the collar, was my mother—a greyer, smaller version of the one who had not aged in my memory.

Lilianna looked at me with tears in her eyes. My mother's eyebrows were raised high in expectation on her wrinkled forehead. I was temporarily frozen in place in the doorway. I could smell the mushrooms cooking in the lasagna; the warm room's volume felt like it had increased with all of the emotions emanating from our individual and collective pains and joys. These women were waiting to see what I would do. My feet moved me forward into the room. Lilianna's eyes told me to go to my mother. For a moment I saw myself through Lilianna's eyes, and then through my mother's eyes. I realized I was becoming a man, that these women had given me my life, and that Rodriguez lived within me, remaining in his body of a young boy as I had matured.

I walked to my mother, kneeled at her feet, and kissed her blue-veined hand many times. I didn't cry, but my heart melted away in my chest, my face felt hot, and my mother's hand was trembling in my hands. Then, as humans do, we reverted to formalities, and we ate, celebrating my birth and our lives. Lilianna sat at the head of the table; I sat to her right; my mother sat to her left. I remember the sound of our cutlery clicking the plates as we cut our lasagna. I recall the sounds of us sipping from our wine glasses. I distinctly remember how deep my mother's mouth lines had etched in around the corners of her lips, running down toward her chin. My mother had wrapped some of my favorite old books in brown paper and tied them in red ribbon. I opened them slowly, ceremoniously. On the title page of The Adventures of Robinson Crusoe, she had inscribed, "Survival is the only teacher." Then Lilianna presented me with a bamboo cage that contained a tarantula, and she said, "This is Rodriguez. He has always been in your heart; now you can take him with you when you go off into the world to become a man. He will listen to you and won't ever judge you."

VI

I HAVE TAKEN RODRIGUEZ with me to college and into my life. I have shared my most intimate, idealistic, and shameful thoughts and feelings with him. My tarantula is the only creature now who knows my whole story.

What I didn't know on the night of that eighteenth birthday celebration was that my mother had cancer and would pass from this world only five months later. She hugged me tightly that night when she parted, for so long that I wondered if she was capable of letting go, and we promised to see each other again, but we never did.

The following year, Lilianna remarried, a very nice man, a baker in a small town in the south, and we rarely saw each other after that, though we spoke on the phone faithfully every Sunday until last year when I received a telegram from the baker informing me that I should come south for her funeral and to collect a box of items Lilianna left for me in her will—a box of

Rodriguez's clothes, his soccer ball, and a very intimate ten-page letter she wrote, in which she addressed me as her "gentle son."

VII

I DON'T KNOW WHY older women have always cared for me and about me. First my mother, for as long as she could bear her pain. Then Lilianna. And now Tonya stood before me, asking to kiss Rodriguez—asking more than she could possibly understand. To kiss my tarantula would be to know things even I wish I had never known. She stood there waiting, and I felt she needed this sign of our connection, this strange healing kiss as a sign of our bond, and I felt my doubts and misgivings dissipate as I fell in love with her tightly drawn face of a mother—the face of all mothers—and I said, "Yes, you may kiss my spider, and may your kiss be a bandage that will heal us both."

Her face relaxed, and she said nothing for a long time as she studied my eyes; and then she leaned in to rest her thin, old lips on my forehead for a lingering kiss.

Photo by Alicia Craven.

Jose Angel Ventura is eighteen years old and from Mexico. He loves his country, his family, and his friends. In the future, he will finish college and go into the army.

My Mexican and American Family and Friends

JOSE ANGEL VENTURA

MY FAMILY AND I moved to America from Mexico when I was sixteen years old. In Mexico, I lived with my grandparents, and in America, I live with my mom and father. I have been in this country for one year so far. I might return to Mexico in two years. My experiences in both Mexico and America—with family and friends—make me who I am.

In Mexico, I worked to help my family at a rock-cutting factory because we needed money. I lived with my grandfather and grandmother because my parents and younger siblings were already in the U.S. I worked because we needed to buy food and clothes, and also to help my family have a better life. My family helped me learn how to work and be independent. I wanted to help them too. Now, in the U.S., I live with my mother, father, my seven-year-old brother, and my sixteen-year-old-sister. In America, it is hard to get a job, but I have more opportunities like school and a better education. I help my parents learn the language. They motivate me when they talk to me about a better life and how to learn English. When my parents tell me to study, I feel more motivation. I want to help my family in Mexico and America and this helps make me who I am.

My friends are important to me too. In Mexico, I had many old friends. We played baseball and we would go to the mall to buy clothes. My friends and I only spoke Spanish, and I played video games with them. When my friends and I were together, I felt relaxed, and connected when I was with them. Here, it is difficult to maintain contact with my friend in Mexico. They are a big motivation for me to return to Mexico in the future—to be with them and my extended family.

In America, I play soccer with my friends. I go to the mall. I have friends who do not speak Spanish and we are in school together. My friends are with me when I have problems, and I help them too, like with homework or when they need advice. I have friends who don't know how to speak Spanish, and friends who speak my language. My friends help me when I don't understand English, and my friends help me understand this country better.

Music is important to me too. The music in Mexico is very good. When I listen to music or when I sing, I feel good. Sometimes I miss my country and my favorite music, mariachi. It is something about my country that I identify with. It reminds me of fiestas with my friends. In America, I want to learn music in English because I think it is very good to listen to. I want to learn what the music is about, learn new words and understand more English. Here, my friends and I have fun listening to English music.

I have lived in both Mexico and America, and my experiences in both countries make me who I am. I want to help my family by getting a good education. When people move to another country, they change in many ways. In Mexico, I didn't have specific goals, just working. Here, I am going to be someone.

Photo by Chet Hay.

Morgen White is nine years old and attends West Woodland Elementary. She is good at climbing. When it rains, she likes to read *Amulet* and play outside. Her biggest adventure happened one time when she was spying, and she got caught.

The Circle of Pollution

MORGEN WHITE

ONCE A BABY FISH was born. When he turned five, his mother said he could play without her watching. His mother said not to go past the black gates. He went out to play. He'd never been past the black gates. Come to think of it, his mother never told him what happened behind the gates. He took one swish forward.

"Should I do it?" said Tim The Fish. Then he saw an orange cap in the water. He thought it was food and took a big swish forward under the gate. He swam 'til he ate the cap, and when he turned around, he was swallowed by a bird. The bird started to head home, and then a bigger bird came and bit the bird on the wing. The bird fell, and before he reached the ground, a bigger bird opened its beak and ate the smaller bird and then flew to the barn. Then Bam! The bird fell to the ground, and a man named Crool picked the bird up by the neck and showed his manager. Then the manager sold the bird to a man named Sam.

Sam ate the bird that night. He choked that night, and died.

Robert Dugoni, a former attorney, is the *New York Times* best-selling author of the David Sloane legal thriller series including *The Jury Master* and *Murder One*, as well as the novel *Damage Control* and the award winning nonfiction expose, *The Cyanide Canary*. He lives in Washington State with his very understanding wife, Cristina, and two terrific children. He teaches the craft of writing across the United States, Canada, and Mexico.

Blink of an Eye

ROBERT DUGONI

I HEARD THE SPRAY of the shower through the closed door, reached to turn the knob, and found it locked. That three-inch-thick piece of wood never seemed so solid, so impenetrable a barrier, as it did that morning and I stood there feeling a keen sense of loss.

Catherine had always taken to the shower in our master bedroom. There's a bathroom just outside her bedroom door, but for some unknown reason that tile-and-grout, tub-and-shower combo just wasn't the same as Mom and Dad's.

My wife entered the room looking harried and concerned, as was the case every morning when we navigated the ritual of getting the kids up and out the door for school. I know marriage counselors blame failed marriages on finances, infidelity, and religious differences, but I'm convinced the morning ritual has contributed to its fair share as well. That morning was particularly stressful because it was one of those weird "in-service" days for the teachers, which meant the kids would be getting out of school early and my wife and I needed to coordinate pick-up, as well as discuss my son's request to see a movie with his friends in the afternoon.

"What are you doing?" she asked.

"The door's locked."

She walked to where I stood and jiggled the handle, as if I were incapable of determining for myself whether a door was truly locked.

"Catherine?" she called out, then with her mouth pressed closer to door. "Catherine!"

There are times when I can just sit and listen to my daughter's squeaky little voice, as entranced by the melody as if listening to beautiful music. This was not one of those moments.

"What!"

"You locked the door."

"What?"

"Unlock the door! Daddy has to get ready for work and we're late. You need to eat breakfast."

I heard the lock click and my wife pulled open the door, fanning the steam. "Have you gone over your spelling words?"

I did not immediately enter, unconvinced my eight year-old had locked the door by mistake. My wife stepped out to make room for me. Our house was built in the 1960s and for some reason the architect decided that a bathroom the size of a postage stamp would suffice. The term master bathroom has never been so misleading.

"Go ahead," she said, looking at me with bewilderment, impatience creeping into her tone.

I stepped in and turned to the small alcove with the sink, wiped a hole in the condensation that covered the mirror, and began to shave, my daughter hidden behind the shower curtain.

"Baby," I called out.

"Yeah," she squeaked.

"Why did you lock the door?"

After a moment's hesitation she said, "I don't know," reconfirming my suspicion it had not been an accident.

The spray of the shower ceased, the buzz of my electric razor pronounced as I guided it across my face. In the cleared spot of the mirror I watched a tiny, tanned arm reach from behind the curtain and pull one of the powder-blue towels from the aluminum bar. A moment later, when Catherine materialized, she looked to be the same little girl I had awakened that morning with a kiss on the cheek, but I knew she was not. She had wrapped the blue towel tightly around her body, her shoulders and head sticking out one end, her legs up to her shins out the other.

"You need to get going," I said. "Mom's getting upset. Do you have your school clothes?"

"No," she said. I noticed her discarded garments on the bathroom floor—not pajamas, but the same clothes she had worn the previous day, a pair of sweatpants with the word NIKE across the seat and the brown t-shirt from a horse back trip to Idaho.

"Did you sleep in your clothes again?"

Her eyebrows arched and her eyes widened, lips spreading into an impish grin. "Maybe."

"Catherine," I said, and she broke out in her unique little laugh.

I tell people my son, Joe, is my conscience, reminding me when my behavior strays off course. Catherine, on the other hand has always been my angel. She melted my heart the moment my wife gave that final push and Catherine entered this world. But her birth also filled me with a sense of dread I never felt with the birth of Joe. The two experiences, so similar in many respects, left completely different impressions. Joe was born early morning after a very long labor. The doctor placed him on his mother's stomach and turned to me as if I were an actor who had just missed his cue to deliver the most important line in the show. When I still didn't get the message, his eyes widened and he gently flicked Joe's engorged testicles.

I got the hint. "It's a boy!" I blurted, perhaps better late than never.

But, of course, there had been none of that with Catherine. In addition to the difference in genitalia, she came into this world at a reasonable hour in the evening after a reasonable labor, her face scrunched as if annoyed at the whole birthing process. Whereas her brother had blonde curls and rosy skin, a mat of black hair covered the crown of Catherine's head, her face round as a ball and her complexion, olive. She looked like my ninety five-year-old Italian grandmother, Nonie.

When I held her in the palms of my hands I remember having to sit, feeling light headed with the thought this was not just anyone's little girl. This was my little girl. I had heard the adage—you know, the one about when you have a boy you only have to worry about one penis, with a daughter you have to worry about a hundred. But that night I realized the truth amidst the humor. I realized it again that morning when I reached to find the bathroom door locked.

"I'll get your clothes," I said and started down the hall to her room. My wife intercepted me, returning to further inspect the troop's progress. "Is she out yet?"

"I'm getting her clothes."

"I told her to bring them in with her."

I shrugged. We were already past that point and I knew it would be quicker to get her clothes myself. What use are dads if not to enable their daughters?

I heard my wife behind me. "I told you to bring your clothes with you."

"I forgot."

"Come on, it's getting late."

As I re-entered the bathroom to deliver Catherine's school uniform, my wife stood yanking at the towel around Catherine's body, wanting to use it to dry her hair, but Catherine held it tight against her body.

"Catherine, darn it, let go."

I handed my wife a second towel from the bar. "Here, use this one."

She took it, rubbing Catherine's head vigorously then stopping.

"Are you getting in the shower?"

"Why don't you get dressed outside," I said, and Catherine eagerly departed, still clutching her towel.

"You remember you have the father-daughter sock-hop tonight?" My wife said as I closed the door.

I didn't, of course, but I stuck to the rules in the man code: never ask for directions and never admit you forgot an event your wife has told you three times to put on your calendar. .

"Of course," I said.

I closed the door and turned on the shower, but did not immediately step in. I considered the black and white photograph framed on the wall, the one of me standing in a shower. On my shoulder, no bigger than a football, is my little girl, her black hair prominent, eyes staring wide at the camera. As the years passed, Catherine continued to shower with me and with her mother, sometimes all of us together. I'd wash her hair, using the shampoo to mold it into a Mohawk or some creation from a Dr. Seuss book, and Catherine would pull back the curtain to giggle at herself in the mirror.

I knew the day would come when self-consciousness, and self-awareness would replace that child's naïveté. The showers had ended well before Catherine turned eight, but that had been my decision; Catherine had showed little signs of modesty before that morning. I also knew this moment was inevitable, as it had been with my son and his mother, and that the day would come when discussions on certain subjects would be better left between Catherine and my wife. I had been warned about the hormonal teenage years when, as my friend Robert explained it, "The aliens snatch your daughter's brain at thirteen, and you become the most embarrassing, annoying person on the planet. Six years later the aliens give it back and you're great again." I think Einstein said something similar.

Still, knowing things would change and being prepared for those changes are not the same, and as I stood in the shower that morning the sense of loss overwhelmed me and I bowed my head, allowing the spray to beat on my neck and wash away my tears.

I RETURNED HOME from my office at close to five that evening. Fighting to meet a publishing deadline, I was squeezing in as many writing hours as I could.

"Did you talk to Mom?" Joe asked as I walked in the door.

"What about?"

"I was at the movies today and I saw all the girls in Catherine's class. It was a party."

"What?"

He told me the name of the little girl who had the birthday. We know the family well.

"Catherine wasn't invited?"

Joe shook his head. "And when her Dad saw me he turned around really quick."

"How many girls were there?"

"A lot, Dad," he said, and I could tell Joe was upset.

They fight a lot, as most siblings do. It's ridiculous, really, given the three-year age difference and the fact that he's big for his age while she's a peanut. But I've also witnessed tender moments indicating they love each other fiercely, and Joe will take on anyone who bothers his sister. It makes no sense, I know, for him to defend her against others for doing the same things he does to annoy her, but whoever said the brother-sister relationship made sense?

I found my wife in the backyard, sitting on the ride mower and wearing a pair of earmuffs. When she noticed me she turned off the mower and removed the muffs.

"Joe told me about the birthday party."

She appeared much calmer about it than I. "I'm sure it was just one of those things where she could only invite a few girls."

"Joe said the whole class was there."

My wife relented, a bit. "Not the whole class... I don't know."

"Aren't they friends?"

"I thought so."

"Does Catherine know?"

"Someone mentioned it at school."

"Where is she?"

"In her room getting ready for the dance."

It broke my heart to think Catherine had been left out, but if the slight had hurt her, she didn't show it. I found her in her room, which she had decorated when we moved into the house. Two of the walls we painted pink with colorful butterflies, the other walls she adorned with pictures of horses, photographs of her in the school plays, and a lot of horse-show ribbons. I'd tell you the color of the throw rug, but we haven't seen it in years, buried under an avalanche of magical clothes, stuffed animals, books, and toys. We say they're magical because no matter how often her mother and I put them away they somehow magically make their way back to the center of the room, and Catherine never knows how it happened.

Catherine stood on her bed swinging her hips and watching the pink poodle skirt with the black and white guitar her mother had sewn swish back and forth in the mirror. She also wore a white sweater, only the top button buttoned, and her mother had pulled her hair back in a ponytail, leaving bangs. She looked like a young Olivia Newton-John in *Grease*.

"Wow," I said, entering. "Don't you look beauteous!"

She smiled and jumped down from the bed, her Mary Jane shoes tapping the one clear spot amidst the mess. She gave me a hug, so excited she giggled. "Hi Daddy."

"You all ready to go?"

"Yep."

"Then I better get changed."

This dance was one of those money-raising events bought at the school auction, when alcohol and guilt force more than one attendee to sign up for things they wake up wishing they hadn't. I once bought a $2,000 trip to run with the bulls in Pamplona, Spain. And I'm afraid to get on a horse! At least it was a tax write-off. But I digress.

Anyway, I had intended to wear a pair of jeans and a button-down shirt. I knew most dads would. But then I thought about my little girl who had not been invited to the birthday party and who was all dressed up and excited to go to the dance with her daddy.

I went to my closet and changed into a pair of khaki pants and a thin black belt, pulled on a t-shirt and slipped into a pair of black penny loafers. In my bathroom I emptied half a tube of gel in the palm of my hand and worked my hair into the best ducktail I could, leaving a small "Elvis" curl in the center of my forehead. As a finishing touch I drew a heart shaped tattoo on my arm with red lipstick and added my daughter's name in the middle. When I emerged Catherine said I looked weird, but did so with a huge smile.

WHEN WE ENTERED the school gymnasium I knew instantly it would be one of those moments that would forever etch itself in my memory, like the night Catherine and I strolled through the twinkling lights of a Phoenix resort, Catherine beguiling in her little blue dress, or the time I sat watching her face light up during a production of *Wicked* at the Ford Theater in Chicago.

Tiny lights sparkled amidst the decorations that had transformed the gym into a 1950s diner, complete with DJ. Catherine never stopped between the entrance and the dance floor. She walked right to the center of the court and held out her hand, my cue to join her. It did not matter that no one else had yet to venture onto the floor or that a crowd stood around the periphery watching. Catherine wanted to dance, and that night she had eyes only for her Daddy, something I was keenly aware also would not last. We crocodile rocked to Elton John and twisted and shouted to Elvis and Buddy Holly, and when the music slowed she stood on my shoes and we swayed to Frankie Valli and the Four Seasons.

When we finally took a break to rest my aching feet we sat off to the side at one of the tables drinking root beer and sharing a large pretzel. Catherine focused on the dance floor but I focused on her. I wanted to tell her not to be in too big a rush to grow up, that life goes by in the blink of an eye. I wanted to tell her that she would only get one chance to be a child, and that when childhood ends, so does that wonderful naïveté that allows us to believe, against all reason, in things like Santa Claus and the Easter Bunny, and gives us the freedom to skip down the street, perform a cartwheel, or burst into song for no particular reason. I wanted to tell her that each year the harsh reality of life steals a little bit more of that naïveté until all that is left is the harsh reality of life. I wanted to tell her that friends will turn their back on her and disappoint her, that girls will plot against her simply because she's pretty and smart, and that boys will say nasty things about her and more than one will break her heart. I wanted to tell her that she'll worry about things like work and finances and mortgages and car payments. Mostly, though, I just wanted to hold her tight, as I used to in the shower, where I could protect her from all the pain that comes with growing up.

But before I could say a word she fell to the side and gripped my bicep, giving it a hug.

"I love you, Daddy," she said.

And I smiled.

I smiled at the way wisdom seems to find us at those moments when we need it most, and because it found me then. I realized it really isn't about what I would tell my daughter at all. It's really about what my daughter most wants to hear, what all children want to hear.

"I love you too, Angel," I replied.

Blink of an Eye © 2010 by Robert Dugoni. Taken from "What I Would Tell Her" © 2010 by Andrea Richesin. Permission to reproduce text granted by Harlequin Books S.A.

Aaliyah Soukup-Stone is nine years old and lives in Ballard. She has six uncles, and her big, fun family lives all over the country. She has a lot of friends—probably over a hundred—from different countries. When it rains, she likes to read fantasy and watch TV with her dog, Bubbles. Her biggest adventure was when she went to Oklahoma with her mom, and she fell out of the really big bed she was sleeping in, but didn't even wake up.

Hiding My Feelings While My Mom Is Busy

AALIYAH SOUKUP-STONE

IT WAS MY first day of school in my new town, Seattle. I, Traya, was nervous.

"I am so scared," I said to my mom.

"I know honey, but you're great at making friends," my mom said. It was true. I *was* great at making friends. I felt better.

As I was walking to the front door of my new school, I noticed three girls from my neighborhood. I thought about the conversation my mom and I had had earlier that morning. Well, I am good at making friends, I thought. Maybe the bullies won't hurt me after all.

"You're going down, Traya!" yelled one of the girls named Ashley.

"Yeah!" repeated her friend Ammie.

"Ha-ha," laughed the third one, Lala.

I miss my old town, I thought.

LATER THAT EVENING...

"Hey, Mom, can I talk to you?" I said.

"Sorry, honey, I'm busy," said my mom. "Maybe later. You know I can't be interrupted because this is a new job." My mom was working on the computer, typing up papers for her latest real estate deal.

"Okay, okay!" I yelled.

My mom was a tall, but tiny woman. She had black hair and dark, soft skin. She was very nice, but when it came to work, she was a little cranky and did not like people bothering her.

THE NEXT DAY...

Bringgg! Kids filed out of the Biglog Elementary School.

"Traya." I heard someone call my name, but I pretended like I didn't hear anything. "Traya!"

"What?" I said, turning around. I saw my teacher, Miss Anderson, with her curly red hair.

"Is everything okay at school? I know you're new," she said.

"Yeah," I lied, and ran to catch my bus.

BACK AT HOME, it was 11:30 p.m.—past my bedtime—but my mom was working so she didn't know I was still up.

"I can't take it anymore," I said to Taffy, my chocolate lab. "I wish I was back in my old town!"

Pop! Wow! A yellowish, greenish light surrounded Taffy and me.

"Traya, what is going on?" said Taffy.

"Taffy, you're talking!" I exclaimed.

"I know," he said back.

Taffy closed his eyes. I did the same. I pretended I was flying in Boxford, my old town. Suddenly there were three pops—*pop-pop-pop*—and I really *was* flying! Then, there were three more pops, and I found myself back on my bed in my new town. Everything was the same, but there was a girl next to me. She looked like my identical twin!

"I can't believe it! I am..." I said.

"Sh. It's dangerous to be magic," she whispered to me. "So don't tell anyone or else you will disappear, and I'll take your place."

"Wow, that's horrible," I whispered.

IN THE MORNING...

I cautiously opened the front door. I gasped at the sight. The bullies, Ashley, Ammie, and Layla were on my front porch! "How did you bullies get to my house?" I asked.

"It is a long story," exclaimed Ashley. "But we're here to say that we're sorry for bullying you. We didn't have any friends, so we thought that bullying would help. Sorry."

"Want to walk to school and play jump rope?" asked Ammie.

"Okay," I rejoiced.

I thought everything would go right, but I was wrong. Here's what happened: We were singing some jumprope songs when I told them about my magical experience from the night before. Then I started to disappear. Everything was white around me. I saw my twin appear, so I ran as fast as I could away from her into the whiteness.

Suddenly, I realized I really didn't *want* to disappear even though that had been my one wish since I had started school in Seattle. I wished as hard as I could that the twin would be gone. I turned around and ran as fast as I could back toward the jump rope. I glanced over my shoulder. My twin was gone! At that moment, I realized that being with my friends was better than being in my old town and being magic.

Stacey Levine is the author of *My Horse and Other Stories* and the novels *Dra—* and *Frances Johnson*; her short fiction collection *The Girl with Brown Fur* was published in 2011. She enjoys reading thrillers.

Milk Boy

STACEY LEVINE

EVERYONE CALLED HIM "Milk Boy" because he was just like milk: thin, rushing everywhere, tinged with blue; he poured himself all around because he needed to; he was nervous and jiggled all day just like a happy little clown, and as a matter of fact, he was a clown, laughing all his life, compromising himself, jerking upon the office floor. But that was just him, this charming Milk Boy who hurtled through the kitchenette to cover up everything with his arms and hands, or any part of himself he could reasonably move or extend.

Embarrassed and ashamed in such a terrible way, and who knew why? No one, really; he ran on his toes, giggling, sad, making a mess of lunch, spreading the backs of his hands on the floor because to be alive itself was an embarrassment, and he wished everyone on earth to forget what they could.

Jumping up because he was simply an active, successful employee, record-keeper, and man, allergic to plants, busy at all times; he raced through the lot to his outsized car, which bloated him along the road home. There, he ran through the hallway to the mirrored door, too touchy to swallow right now or fully speak, let alone to eat a healthful meal of beef, too ashamed to find his gaze, to peek inquiringly into the crevices of his own eyes; and naturally, this charming man was panicked as a rule, though in the future he would certainly own a home and comfortably travel the globe too; but for now, each day was an utter jumble and mess; he could not sleep, but that was just life for this poor, roundabout, clowning, woozy man who, wherever he was, lay embarrassed to death.

He drove to work high across the Eads Bridge, with a little laxative each morning for courage; and he was over-fragile, which never bodes well for office work. He might not last long in life, he knew in the back of his heart. He never had been shown his own strength. But he was too busy all the time to try to understand or calm himself down, for right now he was learning to walk on his hands and juggle on weekends; blazing, leaping through the years, he was jaunty enough to convince himself, making his co-workers laugh, and to suffer was so different from what we ever had imagined.

If only he were a hellion, but he was not. Music made him fall because it was too strong. Once, in the facilities room, he told a colleague he had been born insane, but that it had cleared up. Now gasping, lean, running in long strides toward the elevator door, skidding there, shame the natural color of his hair, he saw his boss Moody Andrews waiting too, so silent, gruff—perhaps it was a problem with bloating or numbness. Then Moody told Milk Boy, woolen-voiced, direct, "I doubt this position is going to work out."

Mightn't anyone feel embarrassed all the time just from being awake or alive, embarrassed, too, at having survived? Milk Boy, all sudden starts and stops, was ashamed by meaning, most of all, and feared ideas of strength. Weren't his legs growing blue? Wasn't he a funny young man, controllable, and so for some girls, cute? Thin as floss, but, in his mind, uncomfortably huge; he could not bear the thought of tales or logs; he always slept poorly, incapable of arousing each morning at the appropriate time, and he never dreamed in pictures.

As the elevator doors opened, he looked down into the metal crack: a rushing, roiling stream lay below. Turning around, he saw his parents, each named Glenn, each enormous, each wearing a plush white robe, and as Milk Boy waved, the elevator doors closed.

To be daring and strong and guileless is best, but he knew he was nowhere near that. The elevator rose. He pressed his chest on his newspaper, rubbing, sliding against the rail, hollering in pleasure or relief; who in the world can explain what this is? "No," he yelled, "I will never say anything dumb again," as Moody, watching from the corner of the elevator, suddenly grew tender, it seemed, smiling damply, pulling his collar, squeezing his boxed drink.

The doors opened on the second floor; there was so much to want. Moody beckoned, "Come to my desk!" as Milk Boy stalled and sweated along the elevator's walls; if he wanted, he could run and run, fast as a dog; and he would be all right sometimes, as when his mother had tucked him in for an hour each night; age twenty-seven or forty-nine, it is so easy for people to tie themselves down; can you imagine, in older age, finally growing calm, knowing, and warm? Then nothing will hurt us again, we think, but we are wrong.

Photo by Chet Hay.

Nazrawit Dessie is ten years old and goes to B.F. Day elementary in Seattle. She lives in Greenwood with her family of five. Nazrawit loves acting, and eighteen is her lucky number. When it rains she likes to go outside and jump in the puddles and read rainy stories on Rainier Street. Nazrawit expects her biggest adventure will be her upcoming four-day field trip to O.P.I. with her class.

Owl

NAZRAWIT DESSIE

ONCE UPON A TIME there was an owl named Pepper. Once, she was on her way to a party and a fish popped out of the river. She had no idea where it came from. She looked around and heard someone scream out, "Ahh, these fishes are not cool." She bent down and looked at the fish. Someone from the party screamed, "Pepper, come to the party!" She looked at the person and looked at the fish. It was dead. She buried the fish so she would not lose it.

She ran to the party, and stopped before she opened the door. She heard people talking inside the bar, so she opened the door but closed it right away, because it was much louder than it was with the door closed. She took her earmuffs out of her purse and put them on. She went inside and looked for a place where it was not as loud as it was in the middle of the bar. When she found a good spot she called her best friend Gahool.

"What do you think of the party?" Pepper asked. Gahool answered back, "I think it's too quiet to be a party."

Pepper's eyes went wide when she heard what Gahool said. Pepper got really mad. She went up on stage, stopped the band, and screamed to the crowd, "It's too loud in here!" One guy in the crowd screamed back, "Of course, it's supposed to be a party!" Pepper was mad and left the party. On her way out she remembered the fish. She walked around and looked for a big bump on the ground. She finally found a bump and started digging a hole. She dug for about seven minutes but could not find the fish.

She went to the store and bought a fishing rod and a basket. She went to a river and went fishing. It was about seven o'clock and Pepper hadn't caught any fish. She went back home and saw that her husband was sleeping on the couch and that there was a box in the kitchen. She asked her husband what the box was. He answered, "It's a surprise." She got confused and opened the box and saw fish! She asked her husband where he got them. He said, "When you went to the party I went fishing." Then she remembered that on her way to the bar she heard someone say, "Ahhh, these fishes are not cool." She asked him, "Were you screaming?" He jumped up and said, "How do you know?" Pepper was surprised and said, "You did all that just for me?" He said, "Yes"! And ever since that day Pepper knew she didn't have to worry about food.

When she woke up the next day, she knew there were enough fish for the day. Her best friend Gahool came and told Pepper that she needed fish. Gahool acted sneaky, like she knew that Pepper had a box of fish. She asked to go fishing, but Pepper knew right away that Gahool knew there were fish. Pepper didn't want to give away her husband's work, so she said, "Let's go fishing."

Right away Gahool said, "How about that box of fish?" Gahool held her mouth.

Pepper said, "That's okay."

Pepper gave Gahool five pieces of fish. She asked her husband if he was mad. But her husband didn't know, so he said "No." Then Pepper explained everything, and her husband turned that no around and made it a "Yes."

Barbara Earl Thomas is a Seattle-based painter and writer, and the executive director of the Northwest African American Museum.

The Mail

BARBARA EARL THOMAS

IT WAS THE ORDER of things that drew her attention, what she first noticed upon entering a room. How a couch met the wall, light falling into right angles disturbed by piles of clothing, stacks of paper, books and magazines or the lack of them spoke to her about what went on in a room. She believed there was a right place for everything, a proper way to view an object that was linked to the universe that ultimately kept everything under control. When things were out of place people could become disturbed and upset. When her parents argued, or seemed unhappy, which they were on occasion, she imagined it was because something, somewhere, was out of place. Everywhere she seemed to find proof of it. She herself could not sleep unless her bedroom was in complete order. Clothes left out, untidy piles, or closet doors left ajar transformed themselves after the lights were out into phantom beings and ominous voids.

Put your clothes away, pick that stuff up off the floor, wash your hands before you touch that food, her parents were always telling her. Even before she could write she was keeping lists in her head, memorizing the order and finding patterns in seemingly random collections of this and that so she could keep ahead of it all.

SHE WAS NOT MUCH past eight when she first became aware of the mail, and how it came and went. This is not to say that she didn't know what mail was before this time, for certainly she did. But it was in her eighth year that its particular pattern, regularity, and relationship to her life first revealed itself to her.

She could not remember exactly when it was, but she found herself noticing how her father entered the house each day after work. He was a tall and thickly built man, what people called "heavyset." From looking at him she took *heavyset* to mean someone who was big but not fat. And because she knew that he spent his days working outside as a heavy-equipment operator, where he moved trees and earth around, she thought that his being heavyset had something do with this, so his bigness was probably a good thing.

Each day she watched her father when he arrived home after work. She counted the four long strides it took him to reach the front porch where he paused, checked the mailbox and collected its contents before entering the house. Some days he barely crossed the threshold before he tore into one of the envelopes. Dropping his lunch bucket and coat right in place he might seize upon an envelope as if it were the very shape of urgency itself. Other days, based on what she could not tell, he barely gave the mail a second glance. On these days he would simply gather it, tuck the pile into his shirt pocket, and wait until he had a chance to put down his things before sitting down at the dining room table to sort through that day's delivery.

There was something about the way he held the mail that told her it was important and this was the way that mail should be handled. She liked to watch him cradle the envelopes in his large mitt-like hands. Commanding it like a stack of playing cards, he slapped the pile against the table to even it out, she believed, and to give the stack a more orderly appearance. Next he methodically examined each piece, one after the other, separating them into two stacks. Taking each piece from the top of the main stack, he raised an eyebrow while periodically pressing his lips tightly together before making a determination whether to place an envelope to the left or the right of him. In the end, he reached for the stack on the right to open and sort through its contents, leaving the stack to his left unopened.

After what seemed like an eternity of watching her father sort the mail, she decided one day to climb up to the table after him to eye what he had left. There she found the stack of unopened envelopes. She looked around the room at her mother and then at her father, waiting for one or the other to object or at least give her some instructions as she approached the pile. Receiving none, she proceeded toward the mail. The first thing she noticed was that there seemed to be two or three basic sizes of envelopes. So she started by organizing the pieces according to size. For practice she put the long ones with the long ones and the short ones with the short ones. She examined the stamps and any other markings on the envelopes she could find. She imagined that this was what her father was doing when he initially eyed the stack.

For weeks or maybe months she was content to order and stack the pieces of mail her father left. When finished she would take her mail pile and place it in the basket at the side of the dining room table where her parents kept the leftover mail, forever it seemed, before finally discarding it.

One day when she was no longer content to simply order and stack the mail she decided that she would open one of the envelopes. Again she eyed her parents, waiting for some prohibition or instruction from them before taking this next step. Once more receiving none she selected an envelope and gently tore it open. She tried as best she could to assume what she considered to be her father's mail pose. First she gripped the stack with both her small hands and then tapping it firmly but lightly on the table so as not to bring undue attention to herself, she raised an eyebrow to scrutinize the contents of one envelope after the other. Because she had only just recently learned to read it was hard, at first, to make much sense of the contents.

Although she could only recognize a word here and there she found that she liked the pictures and this encouraged her to press on. Within a few weeks she discovered that there were patterns and that she was able to make sense out of whole phrases like "The Columbia Record Club" or "The Literary Book of the Month Guild," and so on. In ensuing weeks she was even able to decipher some of the instructions. She found to her delight that just like in school there were boxes to check and choices to make depending on what was in the pictures. She excelled in this activity. Following her father's lead she processed stack after stack of mail every week. Sorting, opening, filling it out, and finally making it into neat piles that she deposited down into the basket beside the table.

Now, just like her father, daily she trained her eyes on the mailbox as she approached her house after school. She grew excited when she saw that the box was full. While she often had an overwhelming urge to jump up and grab the new stack from its place in the box instinctively she knew that the order of things was to leave it there until her father came home.

Before long she was following every movement her father made with the mail. On one occasion she observed that his completed pile didn't go down into the mail basket in the dining room as hers did. With this she soon discovered a delicious secret that she thought made perfect sense in the whole scheme of things, which was that her father was redepositing some of his mail back into the mailbox in the morning before leaving for work. As a result, when the mailman came to deliver mail in the afternoon he would take what her father had deposited in the morning. How wonderful, she thought, it's like a circle. All of a sudden she could see it clearly in her mind's eye, the mail coming and going like a giant circle from every house flowing out and in like a tide. With so much movement going on all over the neighborhood she wondered why she hadn't noticed it before.

That evening when doing her mail she held her pencil especially upright. Writing carefully like she had learned in school, she put checks in any boxes she found in her stack of mail. As always if given the choice of a yes or no box, she checked yes. If there were little cardboard decals to punch out, she would remove them with deliberate purpose and place them carefully in what seemed to be the appropriate slot. Once done, she took great care to replace her completed mail back into the envelopes, if provided. But on this evening instead of depositing all of her completed mail down into the basket as was her habit, she left the table taking some of the envelopes with her to her bedroom. On the following morning after her father had left for work, she climbed up to the mailbox. Carefully perching herself on the porch stool, she reached up and slipped her mail in behind his. And then just like magic, in the afternoon when she returned she found that all the old mail was gone and new mail took its place.

She was ecstatic! For her, the fact that the mailman had taken her pieces of mail away with that of her father's was a sign that she had indeed completed her mail correctly. In her mind she saw herself as doing her part in the immense circular movement of the mail. With each new deposit she grew more confident in her mail-handling abilities. Soon she tackled the entire assortment of mail in the basket next to the dining room table.

One day not long after she had implement her new regime, she heard her father asking her mother in a quizzical tone if she knew where a certain set of records had come from. He said, "I can't for the life of me figure out why we getting these books and goddamned records." "And if that ain't enough," he said, "when I called them goddamned fools at the record company and told them to stop sending that crap here, they acted just like I was crazy or something and told me that I had ordered 'em. Well I told 'em that they was the crazy ones and that I hadn't ordered one goddamned thing and if I was going to order something it wasn't going to be *Around the World in Eighty Days*." In the end her parents concluded that it was indeed a mystery and sometimes strange things happened in this world.

All the while the girl dutifully continued to attend to what she had come to think of as her part of the mail, believing that she played a primary role of some grand cosmic exercise. In all of this she never imagined her mail arriving anywhere or that anyone did anything as a result of it other than maybe give a smile for a job well done. To her way of thinking, keeping the mail tide moving was an end in itself. Her reading skills by now were vastly improved as she was at this point half way through the third grade. She could tell because now when opening up the envelopes she could pick through the information more easily. On this particular day when she opened one of her envelopes she read the words she found there. At first quietly but surely to herself she said, "Finger Hut," then she read it again, but this time out loud and more slowly stretching out the sound of the words, F-i-n-g-e-r H-u-t. What could that be? she thought. Letting her eyes drop down to the photo she saw a picture of two people, a man and a woman, smiling at each other and wearing matching car coats with big initials on the pockets. Under the picture the captions read in bold letters "Genuine Naugahyde." Hmm, she thought. She knew that *genuine* meant that something was really real—but *Naugahyde*? Now there was something she had never heard of. But whatever it was, it was "real Naugahyde," which she assumed must be good because it was real. With this assessment she continued undaunted because she knew that bold letters were a sure clue to help you fill in the blanks. So when she came to the blanks underneath the pictures where it indicated size with three choices of small, medium, and large, she put in "large" for the man and "small" for the woman, because the man was large and the woman was small. In the blanks where it asked for initials she stopped briefly because she couldn't imagine why anyone would think that she would know the initials of the two perfect strangers in the picture. Finally she decided that what they really wanted were the initials of the man and woman in her house. So she put her father's initials under the man's photo and her mother's under the woman's. And as always she checked yes when given the choice between yes and no.

209

Several weeks elapsed. In the time intervening she went about her days as usual making small strides and encountering life's regular mishaps: forgotten homework, a report card that should have been better, all the girls in her class that were prettier and smarter than she was. But by now, almost like a consolation for everything, she, like her father, had the mail to look forward to at the end of each day. It was her private secret success. And she relished the moments of concentration and its comforting regularity. While she continued to hear small rumblings here and there around the house from her parents, who were still plagued by getting things they hadn't asked for, the details of their lives mostly remained remote to her.

It happened on a Saturday, she remembered, because they were all home together when the big brown delivery truck pulled up in front of the house. Hearing a knock, her father went to the door to find a delivery man standing there holding a box, a very large box. The fellow thrusting the package toward her father said he had to sign a paper because the package was for him. Her father bit his lip and signed it wordlessly. Carrying the box back into the dining room, her father passed silent glances of uneasy puzzlement with her mother. Surely not another mistake, her mother said, in a low unconvincing whisper. Following close at her father's side she was looking up at the package and wondering along with her parents when she spotted the label. There in large bold black letters she saw the words "Finger Hut." She said it out loud, then again to herself. For some reason the words sounded strangely familiar to her but for the life of her she couldn't say why. As her father tore into the package, an overpowering smell of fresh plastic wafted out from of the box. It was like the smell of a hundred new dolls at Christmas, she thought, only stronger. He struggled with the wrapping, then in one last anxious motion she saw the cardboard box give way as he reached inside and pulled out into the light not a doll but two new camel-colored car coats— one large, one small—each with initials clearly embroidered on the pockets.

She stared at the coats in amazement. Her face flushed hot. With breath escaping her body in a rush she turned to meet her parents' eyes. Locked there, the kaleidoscope of her world took a turn. Stunned and dispossessed of her senses, her shock compounded as she felt the shape of words uninitiated, forming on her lips. Rising up from her throat came something like a laugh, delivered in a high-pitched voice that was not her own she blurted out, "It's Naugahyde!"

Photo by Alicia Craven.

Deeqa Ali is fourteen years old and comes from South Africa and Somalia. She loves her family and watching movies. In the future, she will be a doctor.

My Life

DEEQA ALI

I am from Somalia but I was raised in South Africa.
I am fourteen years old and
We are eight people in my family.
We are loud and fun.

I am from Somalia.
My flag colors are blue and white.
The flag has a star in between the colors.

I am from South Africa.
It has different people, white and black.
It has different buildings.
Like apartments and offices and post offices.
It has cars.

I am from South Africa.
I have a house there.
My house has three windows and a door.
It has three bedrooms and a red door.

It has a garage.
It has a green garden and
Sunflowers and a willow tree
And red roses.
It has leaves on
The wall.

I am from Somalia.
When I left Somalia, my mother and I left my brother
There with my grandparents.

I am from Somalia.
Leaving my brother was hard for me.
Because he was my friend
And second parent.

I am from Somalia.
In Somalia they have war
So they have weapons and gun turrets.

My dream is to meet my brother again.
To see his face again.
It will be the happiest day of my life.
My family will send money to Somalia
To bring my brother home
To our family house.
To sit down and eat.
Together as one family again.

THE END

Advice to Aspiring Writers

TOM ROBBINS

- Read! To be a good writer, you must first be a good reader; moreover, while any number of cookie-cutter drones can crowd around a TV screen, only people who read have a clear sense of themselves as individuals.

- Write! Write everyday without fail, even if it's only for twenty minutes; even if the nation is on red alert, your typing finger has been pinched by a giant land crab, and your grandmother has just fallen out of a third-story window.

- Fall in love with language. If you aren't already tight with language, start taking language out on dates and see if you can't hook up. Remember: *language is not the frosting, it's the cake.*

- Challenge each and every sentence: challenge it for lucidity, accuracy, originality, and cadence (people read with their ears as well as their eyes). If it doesn't meet the challenge, work on it until it does.

- At the end of a writing day, you should feel exhausted. If you're too perky, that's a sign you're writing your story but not sentences.

- It is not enough to describe experience. You must also experience description. Rhythmical language and evocative imagery possess a power of effect that is equal to, and sometimes even greater than, the effect possessed by content.

- Always compare yourself to the best. Even if you never measure up, it can't help but make you better.

- Avoid majoring in creative writing in college. There, you'll be force-fed a lot of rules. Many of them are well-founded, *but* there is only one rule in writing: whatever works, works. The trick is knowing what is working. The best writers seem to know that intuitively. It's actually quite mysterious—and it cannot be taught. It has to be *caught*. You catch it like some tropical disease.

- Never be afraid to make a fool of yourself. The farthest out you can go is frequently the best place to be. (But pushing the envelope has to come naturally, you can't force it.)

- Be patient. Stop worrying about getting published and concentrate on getting better. In other words, focus on the work itself and not on what may or may not eventually happen to it.

- Don't talk too much about your work in progress—you'll talk it away. Let your ideas flow from your mind to the page without exposing them to air. Especially hot air.

o   Since as a writer you'll be spending a great deal of time alone, you will benefit by learning to appreciate the joys of solitude.

o   Writing professionally is work—but it's also *play*. So, above all, have a good time. If you aren't enjoying writing it, you can hardly expect someone else to enjoy reading it. If you don't actually like to write, *love* to write, feel driven and compelled to write, you're better off abandoning literary ambition in favor of a more legitimate career. Trial lawyer, anyone? Cat burglar?

ACKNOWLEDGMENTS

This is our second edition of *What to Read in the Rain* and, like the first edition, it is the product of hard work by many people. They include:

The production team who pulls the book together, meets with hotel general managers, organizes copyeditors, asks authors, manages authors, fulfills book orders, drives the books to the hotels, and generally sits around and has big ideas:

Justin Allan, Teri Hein, Margot Kenly, and Bill Thorness

The adult authors who donated their work for this edition. Some wrote new work especially for this book while others generously allowed us to reprint previously published works:

Elizabeth Austen, Robert Dugoni, Dave Eggers, Karen Finneyfrock, Margot Khan, Mike Lawson, David Lasky, Stacey Levine, Lisa Maslowe, Frances McCue, Brenda Peterson, Tom Robbins, David Shields, Garth Stein, Barbara Earl Thomas, Sam Howe Verhovek, and S.J. Weinberg

The student authors who labored over their stories in 826 Seattle workshops throughout the summer and fall:

Deeqa Ali, Rebeka Berhanu, Isayas Bikila, Nazrawit Dessie, Kaiz Esmail, Estefani, Ben-Oni Eliezer Jean, Laura Lichtenstein, Zoë Newton, Kidus Solomon, Aaliyah Soukup-Stone, Nhut Truong, Jose Angel Ventura, Samuel Wade, Kaley Walgren, and Morgen White

The workshop teachers, their assistants, and the 826 Seattle classroom tutors who support our students in telling their stories.

The book designer: Jacob Covey

The copyeditors: Angela Jane Fountas, Ann Senechal, and Bill Thorness

People and organizations who supported this project by allowing us

ACKNOWLEDGMENTS

copyright permission: Boeing Museum of Flight for the historic photos in "Jet City," Seattle Art Museum for cooperating in the use of Victoria Haven's art, Henry Alva and Jonas Seaman for the use of their fine photography on our covers.

Seattle artist Victoria Haven, whose place-inspired "Northwest Field Recordings" appear on the three opening sections of the book. Victoria's work has been featured in exhibits at New York's Drawing Center, the Austin Museum of Art and the Seattle Art Museum and has been written about in several publications. Portland's Publication Studio recently launched a book of her work titled *Hit the North*.

826 Seattle staff, an extraordinary group of very hardworking people:

Alex Allred, Justin Allan, Humaira Barlas, Alex Blecker, Alicia Craven, Michelle DeBruyn, Kathleen Goldfarb, Teri Hein, Jamal Hussein, Peggy Allen Jackson, Willie James, and Leslie McCallum

Supporters who helped fund the publication of this book:

Margot Kenly, Bill Cumming, and Amazon.com.

The hotels in downtown Seattle who took a chance and carried our first edition. Special thanks to the people of those hotels who believe (and rightly so) that a book so intrinsically local, written by children and adults, would enhance their guests' stays. Our inaugural hotel partners were:

Alexis Hotel
Grand Hyatt Seattle
Hilton Seattle
Hyatt at Olive 8
Inn at the WAC
Renaissance Seattle Hotel
Pan Pacific Hotel Seattle
Sorrento Hotel

1959

СССР
ПОЧТА 1 РУБ.

SPACE TRAVEL IN YOUR FUTURE?

Many visitors to Seattle have taken heart knowing they could satisfy all of their space travel supply needs with one stop at the Greenwood Space Travel Supply Company, the storefront for 826 Seattle.

The No. 5 bus from downtown Seattle will drop you at the doorstep and wait for you (well, maybe not) while you stock up on bottles of Gravity, Astronaut Ice Cream and vacuum-packed T-shirts. Alternatively, just jet up and use our free rocket parking (on the roof).

Looking for a unique gift to accompany this book for the folks back home? Definitely try* The Greenwood Space Travel Supply Co.

VISIT US:
826 Seattle and The Greenwood Space Travel Supply Co.
8414 Greenwood Ave. North
Seattle, WA. 98103

*AND IF YOU CAN'T GET TO GREENWOOD DURING YOUR SEATTLE VISIT, LOOK FOR OUR SPACE TRAVEL PRODUCTS ONLINE AT WWW.GREENWOODSPACETRAVELSUPPLY.COM.

DON'T FORGET TO WRITE!

SEND YOUR POSTCARD TO:

826 Seattle, Attn: Book Travel Desk, P.O. Box 30764, Seattle, WA 98113

....

YES, *YOU!* We want you, our readers,
to drop us a note. Let us know where you've
taken our rain-slicked anthology.

Send us a postcard! We want your *Greetings from Georgia,*
Musings from Minot, Hola from Chihuahua.

We were inspired to ask for your stories by this lovely note
regarding our first book:

Hey 826 Seattle! I bought your book when I was leaving my hotel, but I never
expected it would save my sanity. We ended up sitting on the tarmac for hours.
I finished my novel, fished in my bag and... there it was! Reading about Elvis in
Seattle and a giant marshmallow man on the Space Needle saved the day. Thanks!
— David N.

```
Z
L. A
165.
```

....

SEND US A POSTCARD WITH YOUR STORY.

- Make it 50 words or less (plus your contact info)
- We will convene a panel of our most creative writers to
  review all entries
- The best entries will be published in next year's edition

The fine print: Sending your entry constitutes your permission for us to publish your work.